EXPERIENCE
ARUBA

T0006991

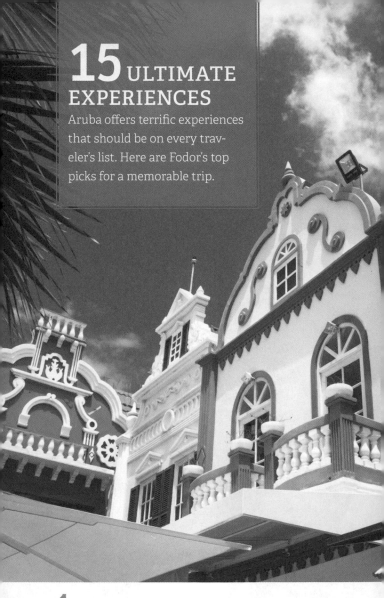

15 ULTIMATE EXPERIENCES

Aruba offers terrific experiences that should be on every traveler's list. Here are Fodor's top picks for a memorable trip.

1 Discover Downtown Oranjestad

The colorful capital is easily explored on foot. Take a Downtown walking tour, and don't miss the beautiful—and free—National Archaeological Museum. *(Ch. 3)*

2 World-Class Beaches

This stunning expanse of powder-soft sand and cerulean sea often tops best beach lists for its sheer beauty and pristine condition. And it's home to Aruba's iconic Fofoti tree, so get your selfie sticks ready. (*Ch. 3, 4, 5, 6, 7*)

3 Glitzy and Glamorous Casinos

If you like to gamble or want to try your hand at a game or two, Aruba's casinos are the real deal, with options ranging from big, glitzy, Las Vegas–style affairs to intimate little gaming rooms. (*Ch. 3, 4, 5*)

4 Stroll the Art Walk

Everywhere you look on San Nicolas's main streets, buildings are covered with beautiful murals. The art walk is free to explore on your own, but guided tours are available through Aruba Mural Tours. *(Ch. 6)*

5 Climb a Lighthouse

This iconic landmark is hard to miss on the north coast. You can climb to the top for wonderful panoramic shots, or book it for a private catered dining experience. *(Ch.5)*

6 Explore Arikok National Park

Aruba's wild side isn't all parties. Join a short free guided hike with a park ranger, or book an exciting ATV safari, a nature hike, or a horseback tour to explore its hidden wonders. *(Ch. 7)*

7 Spelunking in Ancient Caves

Step back in time to commune with Aruba's original inhabitants at Quadirikiri Cave and Fontein Cave with markings from the Arawak Indians. Park rangers offer free guided tours from the entrances. *(Ch. 7)*

8 Visit Paseo Herencia

Located on the Palm Beach tourist strip, Paseo Herencia has restaurants, artisan kiosks, and nightly magical light and water shows in its fountain that make it worth a visit. *(Ch. 5)*

9 Stellar Scuba Diving and Snorkeling

Advanced and novice divers appreciate the plentiful marine life and abundance of wrecks in Aruba's clear waters. There are even guided night dives, deep dives, and shore dives. *(Ch. 8)*

10 Above-Water Adventures

There are plenty of ways to spend time upon Aruba's aqua waves—party day sails, sunset voyages, stand-up paddleboarding, sea kayaking, deep-sea fishing, windsurfing, kiteboarding, and wing foiling. *(Ch. 8)*

11 Dine in a Windmill

The 200-year-old De Olde Molen ("The Old Windmill") was brought from Holland in 1960 and reconstructed piece by piece. You can dine inside, and there's a bar on top, too. *(Ch. 5)*

12 Go Chef's Table Hopping

Aruba has an abundance of chef's table experiences, from typical horseshoe, open-kitchen venue affairs to secret-garden escapes and patio samplings. The culinary talent on this island can keep up with the world's best.

13 Go Barhopping in Buses

Aruba's crazy barhopping buses offer a wild ride replete with stops at local night spots to give visitors a real feel for island partying. The bright red Kukoo Kunuku buses also offer happy hour tours. *(Ch. 2)*

14 Swim at the Natural Pool

Conchi, Arikok Park's stunning natural pool, is only accessible by guided jeep tour, hike, or horseback to preserve the nature around it. Snorkeling in it is surreal; equipment is supplied. *(Ch. 7)*

15 Recharge in Superb Spas

Ultimate treatments in pampering abound in world-class indoor and outdoor spa venues; there's even a floating spa and massages offered in a pool. Many spas use locally sourced ingredients like aloe. *(Ch. 8)*

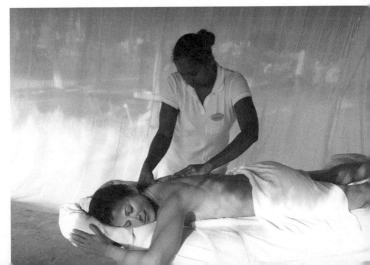

WHAT'S WHERE

1 **Oranjestad.** Aruba's capital is a great place to go for shopping, restaurants, and nightlife.

2 **Eagle, Druif, and Manchebo beaches.** The island's low-rise hotel area offers miles of beautiful beach, and the vibe is laid-back and low-key.

3 **Palm Beach, Noord, and Western Tip.** The island's high-rise hotels are found in Palm Beach in the district of Noord, a very action-packed region. The quieter, more remote Western Tip is anchored by the California Lighthouse.

4 **Savaneta and San Nicolas.** The tiny fishing village of Savaneta was the first Dutch capital on Aruba and now holds some exclusive stays and dining surprises, while San Nicolas, once headquarters of the island's oil industry, has been totally reborn with public art.

5 **Arikok National Park and Environs.** Nearly 20% of Aruba is covered by this sprawling national park. The small town of Santa Cruz in the interior gives a sense of local color and character.

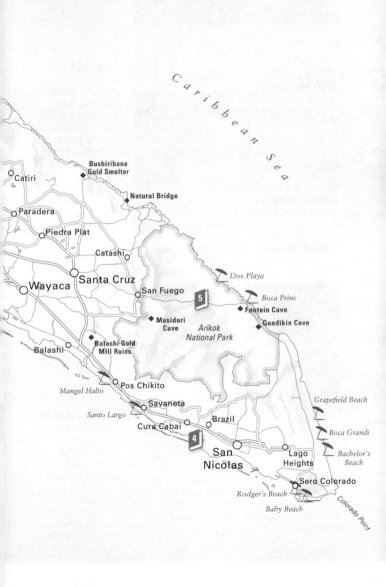

C a r i b b e a n   S e a

○ Catiri

◆ Bushiribana
  Gold Smelter

◆ Natural Bridge

○ Paradera

○ Piedra Plat

○ Catashi

Wayaca ○

Santa Cruz ●

○ San Fuego

5

Dos Playa

Boca Prins

◆ Fontein Cave

◆ Masiduri
  Cave

*Arikok
National Park*

◆ Guadikin Cave

◆ Balashi Gold
  Mill Ruins

Balashi ○

○ Pos Chikito

Mangel Halto

○ Savaneta

Santo Largo

○ Cura Cabai

4

○ Brazil

San
Nicolas ●

○ Lago
  Heights

Grapefield Beach

Boca Grandi

*Bachelor's
Beach*

● Sero Colorado

Rodger's Beach

Baby Beach

Colorado Point

Aruba's Best Beaches

ARASHI BEACH
On the island's northwestern tip, Arashi Beach has a beach bar and restaurant, some *palapas* (thatch shelters), chair rentals, an outdoor shower, and occasional live music.

BABY BEACH
Named for its shallow calm waters and baby-powder-soft sand, the beach's breakwater and unique double reef make it great for kids or snorkeling; snorkel gear, lounge chairs, and sunshade tents can be rented. Look for sea turtles.

BOCA CATALINA
Just north of Palm Beach, this little cove is easily accessible by car or public bus. The crystalline water makes it a favorite with snorkelers; there are a few public shade palapas, but no facilities.

RODGER'S BEACH
A lovely, secluded oasis close to Baby Beach, it's reached only by a secret stairway recently bedecked with mosaic art. There are no facilities, but unless it's a weekend, chances are your only company will be a few little fishing boats.

DOS PLAYA
It's not a swimmable spot, but Dos Playa's two beaches, separated by a swath of limestone, are ideal for sunbathing. It's part of Arikok National Park so there's an entrance fee, but no facilities.

MANGEL HALTO
One of Savaneta's secret snorkel spots, this little cove has soft white sand between lush mangrove forests. There are no facilities, but there are a few nearby restaurant–bars, and a few public shade palapas.

Mangel Halto

EAGLE BEACH
Consistently listed as one of the world's best beaches, the stunning alabaster sand meets an ever-changing wave of cerulean-hued ocean. There are a few stretches with motorized water sports, but it's best for romantic walks and sunset viewing.

PALM BEACH
Studded with high-rise hotels, entertainment venues, and tourist attractions of every ilk, this is Aruba's best-known beach.

Its shallow, clear, pond-calm surf and soft white sand also make it one of the island's best for water sports and young children.

DRUIF BEACH
This lovely half-mile stretch of sand is the main beach for the Divi Aruba All-Inclusive property. Wave action is medium, making it good for children, though the surf is restless at times. There's a public beach bar and plenty of food and drink options in the Alhambra mall.

SURFSIDE BEACH
This could almost be called an urban beach, as it's very near Downtown Oranjestad. There are chair and umbrella rentals, the small Surfside Beach Bar with changing facilities, and lovely sunset views.

BOCA GRANDI
Just outside of San Nicolas, this is the island's best kiteboarding spot, but it's not really a swimmers' beach. There are no facilities or shade palapas, so bring your own food, drink, and beach towel.

Aruba's Best Outdoor Activities

SNORKEL OR SEA KAYAK

With calm, clear aqua waters teeming with tropical fish, there's plenty to see under the waves, including numerous shipwrecks. Sea kayaking is extra special when you go in glass-bottomed boats around the mangroves in Mangel Halto.

GREAT GOLFING

Whether you're learning the game or already love it, Aruba has some great courses including the Robert Trent Jones Jr.–designed Tierra del Sol, the island's premiere 18-hole golf course.

OFFBEAT BLOKARTING

Aruba's constant winds and abundance of flat land make it one of the few places where you can try blokarting (a.k.a. land sailing); Aruba Active Vacations is the only operator to offer it. Prepare to get dusty and dirty; wear sunglasses.

EXPLORE BY BIKE

There are paved Linear Parks along the coast with rentable bike kiosks that make cycling easy. Mountain biking and guided mountain bike tours of the rugged interior are also popular.

WINDSURFING AND KITEBOARDING

With shallow waters and constant gentle winds, the conditions at Fisherman's Huts Beach—also known as Hadicurari Beach—are ideal for beginner windsurfers. Boca Grandi is a favorite hangout for kiteboarders.

DEEP-SEA FISHING

Chartered boats are available for half- or full-day excursions to catch everything from barracuda to tuna.

Windsurfing and kiteboarding

SCUBA DIVING

Aruba is known among divers as the Caribbean's wreck capital, and there are plenty of dive sites right offshore—some in very shallow water—that have helped the island earn its reputation. The island also has plenty of dive operators for novice and expert divers.

OFF-ROADING EXPLORATIONS

Aruba's rugged and rocky interior is best explored with guided ATV or UTV tours, especially if you want to explore the cacti-studded countryside or visit incredible landmarks like the small natural bridges, the gold mine ruins, or the wild coast. Tours can be booked with many major island operators.

ARIKOK PARK HIKING

Explore the island's arid outback with a guided tour to unearth all the secrets of the park. Start at the park's visitor center; there's a small museum, café, and maps, and it's where the free (but short) ranger-guided tours of the immediate area leave from.

HORSEBACK RIDING

Most of Aruba's fine steeds are descendants of the Paso Fino breed (meaning fine step) that the Spanish left behind. There are many guided horseback tours through the island's interesting desert terrain and wild seacoasts.

Aruba with Kids

DE PALM ISLAND

There's great fun for children at this all-inclusive private island, it's like a mini theme park. With a water park, great snorkeling, banana boat rides, and so many sea-themed activities, kids will never want to leave.

ANIMAL SANCTUARIES

Philip's Animal Garden and Donkey Sanctuary Aruba are two important nonprofit organizations that help animals in need, and children will enjoy running around and interacting and feeding the residents at both.

PASEO HERENCIA MALL

This alfresco mall has a gorgeous children's carousel, a mini train for toddlers, a bouncy castle, and free synchronized light and water shows several times per evening. It has frequent free cultural shows, too.

THE BUTTERFLY FARM

An enchanting experience for all ages, this lush tropical garden contains hundreds of colorful winged wonders flying freely and a chrysalis wall, too. Guided tours are included, and admission is good for return visits.

ATLANTIS SUBMARINES

Younger children will enjoy a sea voyage on the semi-submersible so they can run around on the deck, and older children will enjoy diving deep in a real submarine. Both take you to see the *Antilla* shipwreck.

SAIL AND SNORKEL TRIPS

There's no age limit to board the party boats that stop at popular snorkel spots, but they're better for children old enough to swim. Older kids will love the pirate-themed ones with rope swings over the water.

WINDSURFING AND KITEBOARDING

At Hadicurari Beach, children as young as eight can take windsurfing lessons with pro instructors, and older kids can learn to wing foil or kiteboard. Aruba has excellent conditions for these water sports.

There are about 100 donkeys at the Donkey Sanctuary Aruba.

CASIBARI ROCKS
The huge prehistoric boulders of Casibari have stairs and tunnels with railings carved into them so that children can climb to the top and explore them throughout. They resemble Bedrock from *The Flintstones*.

MODERN CINEMA
Aruba has two state-of-the-art cinema complexes in the tourism region: Renaissance Marketplace has a video arcade, and The Movies @ Gloria in Eagle Beach has a stand-alone bouncy park for children.

KIDS' CLUBS
Almost every major resort has a kids' club that offers supervised activities like treasure hunting on the beach or even making their own teddy bears. Some are free, but even with a fee, they are well worth it.

Aruba Today

Arubans are proud of their autonomous standing within the Kingdom of the Netherlands, and Gilberto François "Betico" Croes is heralded as the hero behind the island's *status aparte* (separate status). His birthday, January 25, is an official Aruban holiday.

During the Dutch colonial expansion of the 17th century, Aruba and five other islands—Bonaire, Curaçao, St. Maarten, St. Eustatius, and Saba—became territories known as the Netherlands Antilles, which were later dissolved in 2010.

After World War II these islands began to pressure Holland for autonomy, and in 1954 they became a collective self-governing entity under the umbrella of the Kingdom of the Netherlands.

At that time, several political parties were in power on the island. Soon, however, Juancho Irausquin (who has a major thoroughfare named in his honor) formed a new party that maintained control for nearly two decades. Irausquin was considered the founder of Aruba's new economic order and the precursor of modern Aruban politics. After his death, his party's power diminished.

In 1971 Croes, then a young ambitious school administrator, became the leader of another political party. Bolstered by a thriving economy generated by Aruba's oil refinery, Croes spearheaded the island's cause to secede from the Netherlands Antilles and to gain status as an equal partner within the Dutch kingdom. Sadly, he didn't live to celebrate the realization of his dream. On December 31, 1985, the day before Aruba's new status became official, Croes was in a car accident that put him in a coma for 11 months. He died on November 26, 1986. Etched in the minds of Arubans are his prophetic words: *Si mi cai na cominda, gara e bandera y sigui cu e lucha* (If I die along the way, seize the flag and go on with the struggle).

On March 18, 1948, the Aruban politician Shon A. Eman put forth the first formal proposal for Aruba's independence from the Netherlands Antilles. Twenty-eight years later to the day, Croes declared the first National Anthem and Flag Day, a national holiday that celebrates Aruba's independence with parades, cultural events, and lots of food. Most shops, gas stations, and supermarkets are closed or close early.

Aruba has its own democratic constitution, and its capital is in Oranjestad. The parliament consists of 21 elected members; the majority parties form a seven-member Council of Ministers that's headed by a prime minister for a four-year term. The reigning monarch of the Netherlands appoints a governor, who holds office for a six-year term and acts as her representative. In 2017, Aruba made history in appointing its first female prime minister, Evelyn Wever-Croes.

Today, the country is stable, and the struggle is more about preserving the island's environmental legacy. Welcoming over 2 million visitors a year has taken a toll on the island's fragile ecosystem, and the government has been aggressive in passing laws to protect it. As of 2017 plastic bags were banned, and as of January 2019 plastic straws and cutlery and Styrofoam takeaway containers and plates were also legally banned. The use of sunscreen that contains oxybenzone, which is very harmful to the coral reefs, is also against the law.

Understanding Local Eats

Arubans like their food spicy, and that's where the island's famous Madame Janette sauce comes in handy. It's made with Scotch bonnet peppers (similar to habanero peppers), which are so hot, they can burn your skin when they're broken open. Whether they're turned into *pica* (a relish-like mixture made with papaya) or sliced thin into vinegar and onions, these peppers are sure to set your mouth ablaze. Throw even a modest amount of Madame Janette sauce into a huge pot of soup and your taste buds will tingle. (Referring to the sauce's spicy nature, Aruban men often refer to an attractive woman as a "Madame Janette.")

■ TIP➜ To tame the flames, don't go for a glass of water, as capsaicin, the compound in peppers that produces the heat, isn't water-soluble. Dairy products (especially), sweet fruits, and starchy foods such as rice and bread are the best remedies.

If you're interested in tasting other food that's unique to the Dutch- and Caribbean-influenced island, then you ought to try one of these local treats.

Balashi: After a day at the beach there's nothing better than sipping a nice cold Balashi, Aruba's national beer and the only beer brewed on the island. The taste of Balashi is comparable to a Dutch pilsner.

Bitterballen: Crispy bite-size meatballs, which are breaded and then deep-fried, make for the perfect savory snack or appetizer. Dip them in a side of mustard and wash them down with a cold beverage.

Cocada: Bite-size pieces of these sweet coconut candies are typically served on a coconut shell.

Funchi: This classic Aruban cornmeal side dish is eaten at all times of day and is commonly served with soup.

Keshi Yena: A traditional Aruban dish made with chicken, beef, or seafood in a rich brown sauce of spices and raisins, keshi yena is served with rice in a hollowed-out Gouda cheese rind.

Kesio: This popular dessert is essentially a custard flan or crème caramel.

Pan Bati: The slightly sweet pancakes are commonly eaten as a side with meat, fish, or soup entrées.

Pan Dushi: Delectable little raisin bread rolls are *dushi,* which is Papiamento for "sweet."

Pastechi: Aruba's favorite fast food is an empanada-like fried pastry filled with spiced meat, fish, or cheese.

Carnival

From New Year's Day to the first week in March, Aruba offers its biggest cultural celebration, incorporating local traditions with those of Venezuela, Brazil, the Netherlands, and North America. Trinidadians who came to work at the oil refinery in the 1940s introduced Carnival and steel-pan music to the island; the instruments were originally made from old oil drums.

The monthlong celebration swings between Downtown Oranjestad and the Carnival Village in San Nicolas with pageants, parades, musical competitions, ceremonies, and gala concerts. Local dressmakers turn out the best costumes for parade days as well as the annual carnival queen competition and pageants.

Locals look forward to the Lighting Parade, a nighttime parade held in February that lights up the streets. During the weeks in-between, Aruba has many street parades, locally called "jump-ups," that lead up to the major parade in early March, including San Nicolas's Jouvert Morning Jump-Up (also called the Pajama Party, since it begins at 4 am and many people come straight from bed).

The Grand Parade, as it's called, is held on the Sunday before Ash Wednesday for two days, first in San Nicolas and then in Oranjestad, with thousands dancing in the streets and viewing the floats, costumes, and bands; it's the largest and longest Carnival parade held on the ABC islands. In recent years, the Grand Children's Parade has become one of the most popular and celebrated events, with hundreds of kids and their proud families and friends.

All events end on Shrove Tuesday: at midnight an effigy of King Momo (traditionally depicted as a fat man) is burned to signal the end of the season. For event schedules visit Aruba's official website ⊕ *www.aruba.com*.

Aruba Shopping 101

Of course, there are typical souvenir choices in Aruba like baseball caps, refrigerator magnets, T-shirts, and key chains, but if you take the time to look, you can find items that were made on Aruba. Seek out the Local Market (a stand-alone area of tents just across from the cruise terminal) in Oranjestad for great take-home items made by island artists and crafters. Or, stop by the nearby ArubaMade mini-mall for locally made souvenirs and local products that are great island keepsakes. There are delicious local eats, too.

The Renaissance Marketplace holds a local arts and crafts market every Friday night from 7–10 pm; Paseo Herencia courtyard has a market Tuesday and Thursday nights; and the Ostrich Farm hosts monthly farmers' markets. Art & Craft Aruba posts local artisans' events on their Facebook page (⊕ www.facebook.com/artandcraftaruba).

Many major resorts also host events where local artisans are invited to sell their wares on their property; Bucuti & Tara Beach Resort holds one every Monday starting at 4 pm.

SHOPPING THAT GIVES BACK

American expat Jodi Tobman moved to Aruba in the 1990s and opened a chain of unique retail stores including The Juggling Fish (⊕ www.arubaswimwear.com), The Lazy Lizard (⊕ www.thelazylizard.com), and T.H. Palm and Co. (⊕ www.thpalmandcompany.com), which can be found in both the high-rise and low-rise hotel sectors. Tobman travels the globe seeking out unique products to stock the stores with—items like home goods, clothing, and jewelry, always with an eye toward handcrafted, sustainable, or arty concepts. But most importantly, these stores are part of a community give-back program called Tikkun Olam—loosely translated as "repair the world" in Hebrew—which donates a percentage of every in-store purchase to a local nonprofit of the buyer's choice.

A SPECIAL LOCAL PRODUCT

This happy island produces some of the world's finest aloe, and it's home to the world's oldest aloe company. Founded in 1890, Aruba Aloe Balm N.V. (⊕ arubaaloe.com) was one of the first companies to create and produce aloe-based skin-, hair-, and sun-care products. There are shops at the airport and all over the island.

TRAVEL SMART

Updated by
Susan Campbell

★ **CAPITAL:**
Oranjestad

♔ **POPULATION:**
30,000

🗨 **LANGUAGE:**
Dutch, Papiamento

$ **CURRENCY:**
Aruban florin (AWG)

☎ **COUNTRY CODE:**
297

⚠ **EMERGENCIES:**
911

🚗 **DRIVING:**
On the right

⚡ **ELECTRICITY:**
110 volts
(same as U.S.)

🕐 **TIME:**
Atlantic Standard
Time (same as the
East Coast)

🌐 **WEBSITES:**
www.aruba.com

Know Before You Go

Should you tip in Aruba? If so, to whom and how much? Can you drink the water? Do people speak English or Dutch? Can you use American money, or should you exchange money? Does the island get hurricanes? We've got answers and a few tips to help you make the most of your visit.

WHAT'S THE WEATHER LIKE?

Aruba doesn't really have a rainy season and it's outside of the hurricane belt—one reason why the island is more popular than most during the off-season from mid-May through mid-November, when the risk of Atlantic hurricanes is at its highest. Temperatures are constant (along with the trade winds) year-round. Expect daytime temperatures in the 80s Fahrenheit and nighttime temperatures in the high 70s. Trade winds blow constantly at an average of 20 knots.

DO AMERICANS NEED A PASSPORT OR VISA?

A valid passport is required to enter or reenter the United States from Aruba.

U.S. tourists do not need a visa to travel to Aruba.

SHOULD YOU TIP?

Most restaurants add a service charge of 15%. It's not necessary to tip once a service charge has been added to the bill, but sometimes that tip is shared between all staff. If the service is good, an additional tip of 10% is always appreciated. If no service charge is included on the final bill, then leave the customary tip of 15% to 20%.

DON'T EXPECT LUSH GREENERY

Aruba is not a lush tropical island, and there are no rainforests. In fact, the island only averages 20 inches of rainfall per year. Beyond the palms transplanted on Palm Beach, there's very little greenery. The interior is arid and desert like, and cacti, aloe, and divi-divi trees are the few plants hardy enough to survive and thrive.

IT'S OKAY TO DRINK THE WATER

Aruba's drinking water is among the safest and best tasting in the world and it comes from desalinated seawater. The local beer is also made from desalinated seawater.

ECO-CONSCIOUS SHOPPING

Plastic bags, Styrofoam plates, and plastic straws have been banned, so bring your own reusable shopping bag (and straw) or buy a souvenir one. Look for Arubiano (⊕ arubiano.com) grocery bags featuring iconic Aruban scenes shot by internationally known local photographer, Damilice Mansur; the company also sells flip-flops and hats with Aruban scenes on them. The bags are made from recycled content, and part of the proceeds are donated to the local Aruba Birdlife Conservation foundation.

U.S. DOLLARS ARE FINE

You probably won't need to change any money if you're coming from the United States. American currency is accepted everywhere in Aruba, though you might get some change back in local currency—the Aruban florin, also called the guilder—at smaller out-of-the-way corner stores and gas stations.

THERE'S LOTS TO DO AFTER DARK

Beyond offering idyllic fun-in-the-sun days on gorgeous beaches, Aruba is renowned for its vibrant nightlife and glitzy casinos, most within easy walking distance of each other. The legal drinking and gambling age is 18.

YES, THERE IS TRAFFIC

Oranjestad traffic can be heavy during rush hour. Allow a bit of extra time if you're trying to get into town for a dinner reservation or need to get to the airport at an appointed time. If you rent a car, expect to have some issues with the island's multitude of roundabouts until you get used to them.

EVERYONE SPEAKS ENGLISH

Most Arubans speak at least four languages— English, Spanish, Papiamento, and Dutch. With the odd exception of domestic staff from Latin America working in the large resorts, you'll have no problem finding someone who speaks English.

ADDRESSES ARE INFORMAL

"Informal" might best describe Aruban addresses. Sometimes the street designation is in English (as in J. E. Irausquin Boulevard), other times in Dutch (as in Wilhelminastraat); sometimes it's not specified whether something is a boulevard or a *straat* (street) at all. Street numbers follow street names, and postal codes aren't used. In rural areas you might have to ask a local for directions, but GPS works well island-wide, too.

ECO-FRIENDLY SUNSCREEN IS A MUST

The sun is very strong, and the trade winds can trick you into thinking you're not getting burned, so sunscreen is a must. However, Aruba has also passed a law against sunscreen that contains the coral-harming chemical oxybenzone, so check that yours does not or buy some eco-friendly sunscreen on-island.

SMOKING

As of 2022, Aruba has banned smoking from most public places, including public outdoor terraces and bus shelters. The smoking age has also been raised to 21 years and older.

Getting Here and Around

Aruba is a small island, so it's virtually impossible to get lost when exploring. Most activities take place in and around Oran-jestad or in the two main hotel areas, which are designated as the "low-rise" and "high-rise" areas. Main roads on the island are generally excellent, but getting to some of the more secluded beaches or historic sites might involve driving on unpaved tracks. Though Aruba is typically a very arid island, there can be occasional periods of heavy rain; it's best to avoid exploring the national park or other wilderness areas during these times, since roads can become flooded and muddy conditions can make driving treacherous.

 Air

Aruba is 2½ hours from Miami; 4½ hours from New York; 5 hours from Boston, Chicago, Atlanta, or Toronto. Smaller airlines connect the Dutch islands in the Caribbean, often using Aruba as a hub; it's a ¼- to ½-hour hop (depending on whether you take a prop or a jet plane) from Curaçao to Aruba.

AIRPORTS

Queen Beatrix International Airport (AUA) is equipped with thorough security, air-conditioning, lots of flight displays, and state-of-the-art baggage-handling systems, shopping, and food-and-drink emporiums. There's also airport-wide free Wi-Fi.

First Class Experience Aruba is the island's only airport VIP service. It's well worth the extra funds to skip the numerous lines (except U.S. customs) and relax in a VIP lounge with complimentary drinks and snacks preflight. They can also greet you upon arrival and zip you through that end as well. Luxury airport transfers are also available.

GROUND TRANSPORTATION

A taxi from the airport to most hotels takes about 20 minutes (traffic depending). It costs about $26 to hotels along Eagle Beach, $31 to the high-rise hotels on Palm Beach, and $21 to hotels Downtown. You'll find a taxi stand right outside the baggage-claim area. Aruba taxis are not metered; they operate on a flat rate by destination.

FLIGHTS

Many airlines fly nonstop to Aruba from several cities in North America; connections are usually at a U.S. airport.

There are nonstop flights from Atlanta (Delta), Baltimore (Southwest), Boston (American, JetBlue), Charlotte (American), Chicago (United), Fort Lauderdale (Spirit, JetBlue), Houston (Southwest, United), Miami (American, Aruba Airlines), Newark (United), Minneapolis (Delta), New York–JFK (American, Delta, JetBlue), New York–Newark (United), Orlando (Southwest), Philadelphia (American), and Washington, D.C.–Dulles (United). Seasonal nonstops from major Canadian cities are available from WestJet, Air Canada, and charter airlines like Air Transat.

Because of pre-U.S. customs clearance, you really need three hours before departure from Aruba's airport. Beyond typical check-in lines—unless you check-in online and have no bags to check—you must also go through two separate security checks and two customs as well. The entire procedure takes a lot of time, so be there early. You can get through a lot faster if you pay for the First Class Experience Aruba service that fast-tracks you through all the lines (except U.S. Customs) and offers you a VIP lounge stay before departure.

Bicycle

Since the construction of the island's paved Linear Park, which lines the coast from Downtown Oranjestad to the airport and now also stretches from Fisherman's Huts beach to Malmok, casual cycling has become a big deal on Aruba. There's a bike-sharing program, Green Bike, that makes it easy to hop on one, or you can rent electric bicycles at Aruba E-Bike Tours. Some resorts offer their guests complimentary coaster bikes and e-bikes to pedal around on as well. E-bikes and electric scooters are also big now with many app-based rental kiosks in major tourist locations.

Bus

Arubus N.V. is Aruba's public transportation company. Island buses are clean, well maintained, sometimes air-conditioned, and regularly scheduled; they provide a safe economical way to travel along the resort beaches all the way

Getting Here and Around

to the Downtown Oranjestad main terminal. They stop at almost all major resorts and are a great way to hop into town for groceries without taking expensive taxis. They run until fairly late at night and later on weekends. If you plan to take multiple trips in one day, purchase a day pass for US$10 at the main terminal in Downtown Oranjestad for unlimited access to all their routes. Drivers give change if you don't have the exact fare (no large bills, though) and accept U.S. currency (but give change in florins). A one-way fare is US$2.60, and you can buy a return (round-trip) to Oranjestad for $5. Return bus fares to San Nicolas and Baby Beach from Downtown are $8. Get all the updated information on rates, schedules, and routes on their website because things change often.

 Car

Driving is on the right, just as in the United States. Most of Aruba's major attractions are fairly easy to find, and there are great maps all over the island to find out-of-the-way spots (mapping apps can also help). International traffic signs and Dutch-style traffic signals (with an extra light for a turning lane) can be confusing, though,

if you're not used to them; use extreme caution, especially at intersections, until you grasp the rules of the road.

GASOLINE

Gas prices average a little more than $1.48 a liter (roughly a quarter of a gallon), which is reasonable by Caribbean standards but more expensive than in the United States. Stations are plentiful in and near Oranjestad, San Nicolas, and Santa Cruz and near the major high-rise hotels on the west coast. All take cash and most take major credit cards. Nevertheless, gas prices aren't posted prominently, since they're fixed and the same at all stations.

PARKING

Parking Downtown can be a challenge, but there is Aruparking (pay-to-park) and free parking behind the Renaissance Marketplace. Aruparking meters accept local and U.S. coins as well as credit cards, but if you're going to park Downtown frequently, it's best to download the Pay.aw app to pay. For updated parking info, visit ⊕ *aruparking.com*.

RENTAL CARS

In Aruba you must meet the minimum age requirements of each rental service. (Budget, for example, requires drivers to be over 25; Avis, over 23). A credit card (with a sufficient line of credit available) or a cash deposit of $500 is required. Rates vary seasonally and are usually lower from local agencies, but shopping for bargains and reserving a car online is a good strategy, regardless of which company you rent from. Insurance is available starting at about $10 per day. Most visitors pick up their rental car at the airport, where you'll find both local and international brands; most companies have offices right across the road from the airport exit, but there are branches all over the island, including at major resorts. Most companies offer free drop-off and pickup at your hotel if you aren't renting a car on arrival. You can ask the concierge of your hotel or the front desk to recommend a local rental if you only want one for a day to tour the island. Opt for a four-wheel-drive vehicle if you plan to explore the outback and go off the beaten path.

RENTAL CAR INSURANCE

Everyone who rents a car wonders whether the insurance that the rental companies offer is worth the expense. No one—including us—has a simple answer. If you own a car, your personal auto insurance may cover a rental to some degree, though not all policies protect you abroad; always read your policy's fine print. If you don't have auto insurance, then seriously consider buying the collision- or loss-damage waiver (CDW or LDW) from the rental company, which eliminates your liability for damage to the car. Some credit cards offer CDW coverage, but it's usually supplemental to your own insurance and rarely covers SUVs, minivans, or luxury models. If your coverage is secondary, you may still be liable for loss-of-use costs from the rental company. But no credit card insurance is valid unless you use that card for *all* transactions, from reserving to paying the final bill. It's sometimes cheaper to buy insurance as part of your general travel-insurance policy.

ROADSIDE EMERGENCIES

Discuss with the rental agency what to do in the case of an emergency. Make sure you understand what your insurance covers and what it doesn't; let someone at your accommodations know where you're heading and when you plan to return. Keep emergency numbers with you, just in case. Because Aruba is such a small island, you should never panic if you have car trouble; it's likely you'll be within relatively easy walking distance of a populated area unless you're in the national park.

Getting Here and Around

ROAD CONDITIONS

Aside from the major highways, some of the island's winding roads are poorly marked (although the situation is improving). Keep an eye out for rocks and other debris when driving on remote roads. When in the countryside, also keep your eyes open for wild goats and donkeys that might wander onto the road. Keep in mind that the animals have the right-of-way by law.

RULES OF THE ROAD

Despite the laid-back ways of locals, when they get behind the steering wheel they often speed and take liberties with road rules, especially outside the more heavily traveled Oranjestad and hotel areas. Keep a watchful eye for passing cars and for vehicles coming out of side roads. Speed limits are rarely posted, but the maximum speed is 60 kph (40 mph) and 40 kph (25 mph) through settlements. Speed limits and the use of seat belts are enforced.

 Taxi

You'll find taxis at the airport and also at all major resorts (ask if you need one to be called). You don't really hail cabs in Aruba; if you need one, just go to the nearest hotel and the doorman will get you one. Your restaurant or bar will also call one for you. In Downtown Oranjestad, taxis are always to be found around the Renaissance Marina lower lobby. Taxi rates in Aruba are fixed (i.e., there are no meters; the rates are set by the government and displayed on a chart by zone) and are posted on the Aruba Tourism Authority website and the Aruba airport website, though you should confirm the fare with your driver before your ride begins. The minimum fare is US$7. There is an additional $3 charge to regular fares from 11 pm to 7 am and on Sundays and some holidays. Be forewarned that taxi drivers will not allow anyone in wet bathing suits or wet shorts in their vehicles.

Essentials

🏃 Activities

Since soft sandy beaches and turquoise waters are the biggest draws in Aruba, they can be crowded. Eagle Beach is the less crowded of the main ones and the best the island has to offer for postcard-perfect scenery. Diving is also good in Aruba; there are many wrecks to explore.

Near-constant breezes and tranquil protected waters have proven to be a boon for windsurfers and kiteboarders, who have discovered that conditions on the southwestern coast are ideal for their sports.

A largely undeveloped region in Arikok National Park is the destination of choice for visitors wishing to hike and explore some wild terrain. But more urban Mt. Hooiberg also offers a fun hike with paved stairs carved within the mountain—the island's second-highest peak.

CASINOS

Aruba has excellent casinos for every type of visitor, from first-time slot players to high rollers. Most are attached to or associated with big hotels or resorts. Player's clubs are available at most casinos. Free to join, they offer special discounts, prizes, and points that can be redeemed for free play; complimentary beverages are offered to players everywhere. There are ATMs at every casino, and U.S. dollars are accepted everywhere; as of 2023, all of the island's casinos are nonsmoking. Bingo on weekends with big prizes is popular with locals at many casinos.

🏖 Beaches

The beaches on Aruba are legendary: the solid 7 miles of beachfront along its west coast are baby-powder-soft, blindingly white sand carpets that smile over vast expanses of clear azure water with varying degrees of surf action. The waters of Palm Beach in front of the high-rise resort strip are typically pond-still placid, whereas the waves on the low-rise resort strip on Eagle Beach are typically restless and rolling. The beaches on the northeastern side are unsafe for swimming because of strong currents and rough swells, but they are worth seeking out for their natural beauty and romantic vistas. You might see bodyboarders and kitesurfers out there, but they are typically highly skilled locals who know the conditions well. Swimming on the sunrise side of the island is best done in Savaneta at Mangel Halto and in San Nicolas at off-radar Rodger's Beach or local favorite Baby Beach, named for its

Essentials

toddler-friendly calm waters. Baby Beach also offers great snorkeling, and sea turtles are often spotted there.

Communications

INTERNET

All Aruba hotels offer resort-wide free Wi-Fi, as do many bars, dining spots, and stores; just ask them for their password when you order or buy something. There are also free government-sponsored Wi-Fi hot spots and zones for tourists and locals, with more to come. Just remember, public networks are not secure.

PHONES

To call Aruba direct from the United States, dial 011–297, followed by the seven-digit number in Aruba. To call a local number while in Aruba, dial just the seven-digit number.

To call the United States from Aruba, dial 0, then 1, the area code, and the number. AT&T customers can dial 800–8000 from special phones at the cruise dock and in the airport's arrival and departure halls and charge calls to their credit card.

Both SETAR (⊕ www.setar.aw) and Digicel (⊕ www.digicel-group.com) offer rental mobile phones, but if you're staying for more than a week, it may be just as cost-effective to buy a cheap phone; even easier is buying a prepaid local SIM and using it in your own unlocked phone. Most U.S.-based GSM and CDMA cell phones work in Aruba.

If you have a multiband phone (some countries use frequencies different from those used in the United States) and your service provider uses the world-standard GSM network (as do T-Mobile, AT&T, and Verizon), you can probably use your phone abroad. Roaming fees can be steep though, and you normally pay the toll charges for incoming calls overseas. It's almost always cheaper to send a text message than to make a call.

■TIP→ **Take advantage of the island's abundant free Wi-Fi and use Internet-based apps for making calls like WhatsApp.**

🍴 Dining

There are hundreds of restaurants on Aruba, from elegant eateries to seafront beach bars, and there's a surprisingly large number of chef's tables for such a small island. You can sample a wide range of cuisines reflecting Aruba's extensive blend of cultures; due to a large number of repeat tourists from the United States, American-style fare is everywhere. Chefs must be creative on this tiny island because of the limited number of locally grown ingredients—beyond fresh fish and seafood, much is imported—but lately, they are getting much better at providing farm-to-fork menus when possible and catering to restricted diets like gluten-free and vegan. In fact, Aruba has become one of the Caribbean's most vegan-friendly islands, with many restaurants adding lots of creative and tasty plant-based options to their regular menus and even creating stand-alone vegan menus.

A return to local roots is also trending in the foodie scene; the authentic Aruban lunch buffet at Elements proved to be so popular with locals and visitors alike that they also extended it to their dinner offerings. And catch-of-the-day including local lobster has authentic local eateries like Taste My Aruba really hopping with visitors every night. Fusions of styles and choices of cuisines all under one roof have also become a thing—the collection of dining spots at the new Cove Mall is like the United Nations, and across the street, Paseo Herencia offers even more international choices.

Breakfast lovers are in luck as most resorts have bountiful breakfast buffets, and you can't go wrong at The Dutch Pancakehouse at any time of day. A la carte brunches (and not only on Sundays) have popped up all over the place; there's even one in a donut boat while you snorkel. Pop-up gourmet catered picnics have also become all the rage (especially for surprise proposals) and gourmet tapas paired with wines or even beer and beer cocktails have also taken root in many spots.

Although most resorts offer better-than-average dining, ask locals about their favorite spots; some of the lesser-known restaurants, snacks, and food trucks offer excellent reasonably priced food worth sleuthing out. Most restaurants on the western side of the island are along Palm Beach or in Downtown Oranjestad, both easily accessible by taxi or bus. Some restaurants in Savaneta and San Nicolas are worth the trip, too.

The island is also a particularly family-friendly destination, so bringing the kids along is rarely a problem, and many restaurants offer children's menus; just make sure there aren't any toes-in-the-sand dining opportunities to avoid any awkward moments.

Unless otherwise noted, the restaurants listed in this guide are open daily for lunch and dinner.

38

Essentials

ARUBAN CUISINE

Aruba shares many of its traditional foods with Bonaire and Curaçao. These dishes are a fusion of the various influences that have shaped the culture of the islands. Proximity to mainland South America means that many traditional snack and breakfast foods of Venezuelan origin, such as empanadas, have been adopted into local eats; on Aruba they are called *pastechis* and come with a wide variety of fillings. The Dutch influence is evident in the fondness for cheese of all sorts, but especially Gouda. *Keshi yena,* ground meat or seafood with seasonings placed in a hollowed-out cheese rind before baking, is a national dish. Arubans also love their *bolos* (cakes), so look for local favorites like cashew nut, pistachio, or chocolate rum cake.

If there's one thread that unites the cuisines of the Caribbean, it's cornmeal, and Arubans love nothing more than a side of *funchi* (like a thick polenta) or a *pan bati* (a fried cornmeal pancake) to make a traditional meal complete. Though Aruban cuisine isn't by nature spicy, it's almost always accompanied by a small bowl of spicy *pica* (a condiment of fiery hot peppers and onions in vinegar) or a bottle of hot sauce made from local peppers. An abundance of fish means that seafood is the most popular protein on the island; it's been said that if there were an Aruban national dish, it would be the catch of the day.

PRICES AND DRESS

Aruba's elegant restaurants—where you might have to dress up a little (jackets for men, sundresses for women)—can be pricey. If you want to spend fewer florins, opt for the more casual spots, where being comfortable is the only dress requirement. A sweater draped over your shoulders will go a long way against the chill of air-conditioning. If you plan to eat in the open air, bring along insect repellent in case the mosquitoes get unruly.

We assume that restaurants and hotels accept credit cards. If they don't, we'll note it in the review.

RESERVATIONS

To ensure that you get to eat at the restaurants of your choice, make some calls or visit their websites when you get to the island—especially during high season—to secure reservations. Many restaurants now have online booking options, but some places are asking for a deposit or charging a fee if the party is a no-show. You may have a hard time finding a restaurant that's open for lunch on Sunday, and some smaller eateries are closed on Monday.

We mention reservations only when they're essential (there's no other way you'll ever get a table, like at intimate chef's table venues) or when they're not accepted. We mention dress only when men are required to wear a jacket or a jacket and tie. Shorts and flip-flops are best left for the beach bars, but casual shirts and slacks and sundresses are welcome just about everywhere. Many indoor spots are heavy on the air-conditioning, so a light sweater or wrap for women or a light jacket for men is also a good idea.

TIPPING
Most restaurants add a service charge of 15%. It's not necessary to tip once a service charge has been added to the bill, but sometimes that tip is shared between all staff. If the service is good, an additional tip of 10% is always appreciated. If no service charge is included on the final bill, then leave the customary tip of 15% to 20%.

WINES, BEER, AND SPIRITS
Arubans have a great love for wine, so even small supermarkets have a fairly good selection of European and South American wines at prices that are reasonable by Caribbean standards. And

though it's difficult to grow grapes in this arid climate, Alto Vista Winery and Distillery is doing a good job of creating its own signature vintages; they also give tours.

The beer of choice in Aruba is the island-brewed Balashi and Balashi Chill, often served with a wedge of lime (both made from desalinated seawater). Dutch Amstel and Amstel Bright run a close second. Local spirits also include *ponche crema*, a wickedly potent eggnog type of drink, and *coecoei*, a thick red-licorice-tasting liqueur that's an integral ingredient in the island's famous signature cocktail Aruba Ariba. Pepe Margo, a new boutique artisanal distillery in Downtown Oranjestad, is producing some new unique island spirits; they also give tours of their facility and tastings.

What It Costs in U.S. Dollars			
$	$$	$$$	$$$$
RESTAURANTS			
under $12	$12–$20	$21–$30	over $30
HOTELS			
under $275	$275–$375	$376–$475	over $475

⇨ *Prices in the restaurant reviews are the average cost of a main course at dinner or, if dinner isn't served, at lunch;*

Essentials

taxes and service charges are generally included. Prices in the hotel reviews are the lowest cost of a standard double room in high season, excluding taxes, service charges, and meal plans (except at all-inclusives).

 Embassy/Consulate

There is no U.S. embassy on Aruba. If you need assistance you must call the embassy in Curaçao. ⇨ *See Contacts.*

➕ Health and Safety

Arubans are very friendly, so you needn't be afraid to stop and ask anyone for directions. It's a relatively safe island, but common-sense rules still apply. Lock your rental car when you leave it, and leave valuables in your hotel safe. Don't leave bags unattended in the airport, on the beach, or on tour vehicles.

As a rule, water is pure—even tap water—and the health and sanitary conditions in supermarkets, hotels, and local restaurants are just like in the United States. But, just as you would at home, wash or peel all fruits and vegetables before eating them. Also watch what you eat, especially at outdoor buffets in the hot

sun. Make sure cooked food is hot and cold food has been properly refrigerated. If there's a need, pharmacies are readily available.

The major health risk is sunburn or sunstroke. Aruba's trade winds can fool you into thinking you're not getting a sunburn. Use sunscreen with an SPF of at least 15—especially if you're fair—and apply it liberally and often. Make sure the sunscreen is water-resistant if you're engaging in water sports. Aruba has a law that sunscreen must be reef-friendly, and legal options are readily available on the island. Always limit your sun time for the first few days, drink plenty of liquids, and limit your intake of caffeine and alcohol, which can hasten dehydration.

Mosquitoes can be bothersome if you're dining outside after dusk, so pack (or buy on island) eco-friendly bug repellent. The strong trade winds generally keep bugs at bay during the day. Zika and dengue have been reported on Aruba, but the island is not considered a high-risk zone. Protect yourself regardless.

Don't fly within 24 hours of scuba diving. In an emergency, air ambulance services will fly you to Curaçao at a low altitude if you need to get to a decompression chamber.

IMMUNIZATIONS

Check out the CDC and the U.S. Department of State websites, both of which have destination-specific vaccine guidance. Also, in case travel is curtailed abruptly again, consider buying trip insurance. Just be sure to read the fine print: not all travel insurance policies cover pandemic-related cancellations. Keep up-to-date on Aruba's traveler's health requirements at their official website (⊕ www.aruba.com/us/traveler-health-requirements).

OVER-THE-COUNTER REMEDIES

There are a number of pharmacies and stores selling medications throughout the island (including at most hotels), and virtually anything obtainable in North America is available in Aruba. There is also a walk-in doctor's clinic at Botica di Servicio on the Palm Beach strip.

RESTROOMS

Outside Oranjestad and the tourism regions, public restrooms can be found in gas stations, fast food outlets, and small restaurants; sometimes a purchase is necessary.

 Lodging

Aruba is known for its large, luxurious high-rise resorts and vast array of time-shares, but it also has a nice selection of smaller low-rise resorts. If you're on a budget, consider booking one of the island's many apartment-style units, so you can eat in sometimes instead of having to rely on restaurants exclusively. Aruba also has Airbnb now, too.

Most Aruba hotels are found in two clusters: the low-rise hotels in a stretch along Druif Beach and Eagle Beach and the high-rise hotels on a stretch of Palm Beach. With a few exceptions, the hotels in the high-rise area tend to be larger and more expensive than their low-rise counterparts, but they usually offer a wider range of services.

Accommodations in Aruba run the gamut from large high-rise hotels and resorts to sprawling condo complexes to small, locally owned boutique establishments—and even luxury villa rentals in well-designed private communities where fractional ownership is also an option. Most hotels are west of Oranjestad, along L. G. Smith and J. E. Irausquin Boulevards. Many are self-contained complexes

Essentials

with restaurants, shops, casinos, water-sports centers, health clubs, and spas. And there are a surprising number of small and economical apartment-style hotels, bed-and-breakfasts, and family-run escapes in the interior if you know where to look. The number of all-inclusive options is growing, and increasingly, big-name-brand hotels are beginning to offer more comprehensive meal plan options. Savaneta now offers overwater bungalows at Aruba Ocean Villas, as well as treehouse stays. Time-shares have always been big on this island, and the Divi family of resorts offers many different options in their various locations.

Large Resorts: These all-encompassing vacation destinations offer myriad dining options, casinos, shops, water-sports centers, health clubs, and car-rental desks. The island also has many all-inclusive options.

Time-Shares: Large time-share properties are also popular, luring visitors who prefer to prepare some of their own meals and have a bit more living space than you might find in the typical resort hotel room, plus fully stocked kitchens with everything you need for cooking … except the food. You can order your groceries online to be stocked ahead at many resorts now, too.

Boutique Resorts: You'll find a few small resorts that offer more personal service and better reflect the natural sense of Aruban hospitality you'll find all over the island. There are some lovely B&Bs as well, including a glam-style camping spot in the desert.

■ **TIP→ Hotels have private bathrooms, phones, and TVs and don't offer meals unless we specify a meal plan in the review (i.e., breakfast, some meals, all meals, all-inclusive). We always list facilities but not whether you'll be charged an extra fee to use them.**

APARTMENT AND HOUSE RENTALS

Apartments and time-share condos are common in Aruba. So if you're looking for more space for your family or group to spread out in (and especially if you want to have access to a kitchen to make some meals), this can be a very budget-friendly option. The money you save can be used for more dining and activities. Many time-share resorts are full service, offering the same range of water sports and other activities as any other resort, and almost all of them offer unused units on their websites (some through third-party booking sites). Some regular resorts also have a time-share component. Airbnb also offers rental options on the island, ranging from tiny cottage-style stays to luxurious stand-alone villas.

RESERVATIONS

When making reservations, be sure you understand how much you are really paying before finalizing any reservation. Hotels collect 12.5% in taxes and there's an additional $3 per day Environment Levy. Service charge is dependent on the hotel.

Some resorts will allow you to cancel without any kind of penalty—even if you prepaid to secure a discounted rate—if you cancel at least 24 hours in advance. Others require you to cancel a week in advance or penalize you the cost of one night. Small inns and B&Bs are most likely to require you to cancel far in advance. Most hotels allow children under a certain age to stay in their parents' room at no extra charge, but others charge for them as extra adults; find out the cutoff age for discounts.

💲 Money

Arubans happily accept U.S. dollars virtually everywhere, so most travelers will find no real need to exchange money. The official currency is the Aruban florin (Afl), also called the guilder, which is made up of 100 cents. Silver coins come in denominations of 1, 2½, 5, 10, 25, and 50 (the square one) cents. Paper currency comes in denominations of 5, 10, 25, 50, and 100 florins.

Prices quoted throughout this book are in U.S. dollars unless otherwise noted.

For purchases you'll pay a 1.5% BBO tax (a turnover tax on each level of sale for all goods and services) in all but the duty-free shops.

Prices throughout this guide are given for adults. Substantially reduced fees are almost always available for children, students, and seniors for activities.

ATMS AND BANKS

If you need fast cash, you'll find ATMs that accept international cards (and dispense cash in both U.S. and local currency) at banks in Oranjestad, at the major malls, and along the

Essentials

roads leading to the hotel strip, as well as in every casino and at the airport.

Nightlife

Aruba comes alive by night, and has become a true party hot spot. The casinos—though not as elaborate as those in Las Vegas—are among the best of any Caribbean island.

For information on specific events, check out the free magazines and island guides you can get at the airport and in hotel lobbies, like *My Aruba Guide*.

Packing

Dress on Aruba is generally casual. Bring loose-fitting clothing made of natural fabrics to see you through days of heat and humidity. Pack a beach cover-up, both to protect yourself from the sun and to provide something to wear to and from your hotel room. Bathing suits and immodest attire are frowned upon away from the beach. A sun hat is advisable, but you don't have to pack one—inexpensive straw hats are available everywhere—but be forewarned that the wind is constant so you might have to tie it or find a firm-fitting one. For shopping and sightseeing,

bring shorts, jeans, T-shirts, cotton shirts, slacks, sundresses, and good walking shoes. Nighttime dress can range from very informal to casually elegant, depending on the establishment. A tie is practically never required, but a jacket may be appropriate in fancy restaurants. You may need a light sweater or jacket for evenings—especially when dining indoors, as the air-conditioning can be set very high in many restaurants. Pack more than one bathing suit and clothespins or towel clips to secure your towel to your lounger, as the wind can be strong on the beaches.

Performing Arts

Aruba has a handful of not-so-famous but very talented performers. Over the years, several local artists, including singer-songwriter Julio Bernardo Euson, choreographer Wilma Kuiperi, sculptor Ciro Abath, and visual artist Elvis Lopez, have gained international renown. Furthermore, many Aruban musicians play more than one type of music (classical, jazz, soca, salsa, reggae, calypso, rap, pop), and many compose as well as perform. Edjean Semeleer has followed in the footsteps of his mentor Padu Lampe—the composer of the island's national anthem and a beloved local star—to become one of the island's best-loved entertainers. His performances pack Aruba's biggest halls, especially his annual Christmas concert. But nipping at his heels are some very talented up-and-comers like indie/alt-rock band Active Mirror, doing their best to make international headway, and Jonathan Thiel, better known as "Jeon", whose own Aruba anthem video is making a big splash internationally, too.

The island's many festivals showcase arts and culture and sports on a rotating basis, with new ones popping up all the time. To find out what's going on, check out the local English-language newspapers or look for events online at ⊕ www.aruba.com/us/calendar.

📦 Shipping

Post Aruba's website has all the information you need for sending mail. From Aruba to the United States or Canada, a letter costs approximately $1.45 and postcards cost about $1. Expect it to take one to two weeks to arrive.

If you need to send a package in a hurry, there are a few options. FedEx offers overnight service to the United States if you get your package in before 3 pm; there is a convenient office in Downtown Oranjestad. Another big courier service is UPS, and several smaller local courier services, most of them open weekdays 9 to 5, also provide international deliveries.

👜 Shopping

Shopping can be good on Aruba. Although stores on the island often use the tagline "duty-free," the word "prices" is usually printed underneath in much smaller letters. The only real duty-free shopping is in the departures area of the airport. (Passengers bound for the United States should be sure to shop before proceeding through U.S. customs in Aruba.) Downtown stores do have very low sales tax, though, and they offer some excellent bargains on high-end luxury items like gold, silver, gems, and high-end watches. Major credit cards are welcome everywhere, as are U.S. dollars.

Essentials

Aruba's souvenir and crafts stores are full of delft Dutch porcelains and figurines, as befits the island's heritage. Dutch cheese is a good buy, as are hand-embroidered linens and any products made from the native aloe vera plant—sunburn cream, face masks, or skin refreshers found in the many official Aruba Aloe stores; eco-friendly sunscreen mandated by law is also available. Local arts and crafts run toward wood carvings and earthenware emblazoned with "Aruba: One Happy Island" and the like, but there are shops with unique locally made items like ArubaMade Mall. Don't try to bargain unless you are at a flea market or stall. Arubans consider it rude to haggle, despite what you may hear to the contrary.

There is late-night shopping in two locations. The first—in Downtown Oranjestad at Renaissance Mall, a multilevel indoor-outdoor complex—stays open until 8 pm, and shops in the modern, multilevel indoor shopping mall off the high-rise strip—Palm Beach Plaza—stay open until 10 pm. Many of the shops around Paseo Herencia also stay open late in high season. A few other shops that stay open late can be found in Alhambra Mall as well. And most resorts have their own shops. Don't expect plastic bags for your goods or groceries, as Aruba banned them in 2017. There are nice reusable bags for purchase all over the place that are made from recycled materials, and some of them are imprinted with authentic Aruba scenes that make them great souvenirs. There are many local arts and crafts markets that pop up on a regular basis all over the island and at the resorts, too.

Visitor Information

HOLIDAYS

Aruba's official holidays are New Year's Day, Good Friday, Easter Sunday, and Christmas, as well as Betico Croes Day (January 25), National Anthem and Flag Day (March 18), King's Day (April 30), Labor Day (May 1), and Ascension Day (39 days after Easter).

WEDDINGS

People over the age of 18 can marry as long as they submit the appropriate documents 14 days in advance. Couples are required to submit birth certificates with raised seals, through the mail or in person, to Aruba's Office of the Civil Registry. They also need an apostil—a document proving they're free to marry—from their country of residence. Same-sex ceremonies are available in Aruba, though they're not legally binding.

With so many beautiful spots to choose from, weddings in Aruba are guaranteed to be romantic. Most resorts have their own wedding planning department or use a local partner, and they can handle everything from start to finish for you. Aruba also now hosts the world's largest vow renewal group ceremony for couples from all over the world on Eagle Beach each year.

 When to Go

Aruba's high season runs from early December through mid-April. During this season you're guaranteed the most entertainment at resorts and the most people with whom to enjoy it. January and February are the most expensive times to visit, both for people staying a week or more and for cruise-ship passengers coming ashore. During this period hotels are solidly booked, and you must make reservations at least two or three months in advance for the very best places (and to get the best airfares). Hotel prices can drop 20% to 40% after April 15. Summer is when many of the hotels and businesses improve their properties, so expect some construction during that season.

Contacts

Air

CONTACTS First Class Aruba.
✉ *Queen Beatrix International Airport, Sabana Berde, Oranjestad* ⊕ *firstclassaruba. com.* **Queen Beatrix International Airport.** ⊕ *www.airportaruba. com.*

Bicycle

Green Bike Aruba. ✉ *Ponto 69, Oranjestad* ☎ *297/594–6368* ⊕ *greenbikearuba.com.*

Bus

CONTACTS Arubus. ✉ *Oranjestad* ☎ *297/520-2300* ⊕ *arubus.com.*

Car

CAR RENTALS Amigo. ✉ *Across from Arrival Terminal Airport and in Oranjestad, Schotlandstraat 56* ☎ *297/583–8833* ⊕ *www.amigocar.com.* **Avis.** ✉ *Queen Beatrix Airport, Reina Beatrix Airport* ☎ *297/582–5496 in Aruba,* *800/532–1527* ⊕ *www.avis.ca/en/locations/ab/ oranjestad/aua.* **Budget.** ✉ *Reina Beatrix Airport* ☎ *297/582–8600,* *800/472–3325 in Aruba* ⊕ *www.budgetaruba.com.* **Thrifty.** ✉ *Reina Beatrix Airport* ☎ *297/583–4902* ⊕ *www. thriftycarrentalaruba.com.* **Tropic Car Rental.** ✉ *Reina Beatrix Airport* ☎ *297/583–7336* ⊕ *www.tropiccarrent-aruba. com.*

PARKING Aruparking. ✉ *Oranjestad* ☎ *297/520-2323* ⊕ *aruparking.com.*

Embassy/Consulate

CONTACTS U.S. Consulate Curaçao. ✉ *J.B. Gorsiraweg 1, Willemstad* ☎ *5999/433–2200,* *301/985–8733* ⊕ *cw.usconsulate.gov.*

◉ Visitor Information

CONTACTS Aruba Food and Beverage Association. ✉ Oranjestad ☎ 297/564–9001 ⊕ www.arubadining.com. **Aruba Hotel and Tourism Association.** ✉ Oranjestad ☎ 297/582–2607 ⊕ ahata.com. **Aruba Tourism Authority.** ✉ L. G. Smith Blvd. 8, Oranjestad ☎ 800/862–7822 in the U.S./international, 297/582–3777 in Aruba ⊕ www.aruba.com. **Papiamento Online Courses.** ✉ Oranjestad ⊕ cudoo.com/?s=papiamento. **Post Aruba.** ✉ Oranjestad ⊕ www.postaruba.com.

WEDDINGS Aruba Fairy Tales Weddings. ✉ Costa Linda Beach Resort, Oranjestad ☎ 297/593–0045 ⊕ www.arubafairytales.com. **Aruba Weddings for You.** ✉ Oranjestad ☎ 297/525–5293 ⊕ www.arubaweddingsforyou.com. **Dream Weddings Aruba.** ✉ Matadera 9W, Noord ☎ 297/587–5991 ⊕ dreamweddingsaruba.com.

Taxi

CONTACTS Arubas Transfer Tour and Taxi C.A.. ✉ Reina Beatrix Airport ☎ 297/582–2116, 297/582–2010 ⊕ www.airportaruba.com/taxi-transportation.

Papiamento Primer

Papiamento is a hybrid language born out of the colorful past of Aruba, Bonaire, and Curaçao. The language's use is generally thought to have started in the 17th century when Sephardic Jews migrated with their African slaves from Brazil to Curaçao. The slaves spoke a pidgin Portuguese, which may have been blended with pure Portuguese, some Dutch (the colonial power in charge of the island), and Arawakan. Proximity to the mainland meant that Spanish and English words were also incorporated.

Papiamento is roughly translated as "the way of speaking." (Sometimes the suffix -mentu is spelled in the Spanish and Portuguese way -mento, creating the variant spelling.) It began as an oral tradition, handed down through the generations and spoken by all social classes on the islands. There's no uniform spelling or grammar from island to island, or even from one neighborhood to another. Nevertheless, it's beginning to receive some official recognition, and anyone applying for citizenship must be fluent in both Papiamento and Dutch.

Arubans enjoy it when visitors use their language, so don't be shy. You can buy a Papiamento dictionary to build your vocabulary, and there are online courses and videos to help you as well, but here are a few pleasantries to get you started:

Bon dia. Good morning.

Bon tardi. Good afternoon.

Bon nochi. Good evening/night.

Bon bini. Welcome.

Ayo. Bye.

Te aworo. See you later.

Pasa un bon dia. Have a good day.

Danki. Thank you.

Na bo ordo. You're welcome.

Con ta bai? How are you?

Mi ta bon. I am fine.

Ban goza! Let's enjoy!

Pabien! Congratulations!

Quanto costa esaki? How much is this?

Hopi bon. Very good.

Ami. Me.

Abo. You.

Nos dos. The two of us.

Mi dushi. My sweetheart.

Dushi. Sweet or cool.

Ku tur mi amor. With all my love.

Un braza. A hug.

Un sunchi. A kiss.

Mi stima Aruba. I love Aruba.

Dushi Tera. Beloved land.

How to Spend 5 Days in Aruba

If you're heading to One Happy Island, you probably intend to spend a lot of time on the beach, but there are some excellent reasons to roll out of that surf-side hammock and explore more of Aruba. Remember that all of Aruba's beaches are public, so you can take a dip wherever you like as long as you have a bathing suit handy.

DAY 1: PALM BEACH PLEASURES

Even if you're staying else-where, **Palm Beach** is worth a visit on your first day to see where all the action is. This area is famous for its water sports and sailing and snorkel excursions, as well as its dining, shopping, and nightlife options. It's safe to walk day or night and compact enough to discover on foot. Plan a snorkel excursion for the morning, followed by lunch at one of the many beachfront cafés or pier bars. After lunch, head to the pristine stretch of sand in front of the Holiday Inn for some beach time; floats can be rent-ed at one of the beach kiosks.
■ TIP➔ There are digital lockers on the beach between the Holi-day Inn and MooMba Beach Bar to store any valuables.

After dark, right across the street, don't miss the colorful free nightly water shows at **Paseo Herencia** or the cornucopia of nightlife and din-ing at **The Cove Mall,** including the trendy rooftop hotspot **The Vue.** Afterward, head to "The Strip" to find scads of casual and no-reservation-required eating and drinking spots. There are lots of open-air kiosks for shopping on the strip, and you'll also be close to many of the resort casinos.

LOGISTICS

Accessible by public bus or taxi, or simply drive along Route 1B, which runs along the coast from tip to tip. (1A is northbound, 1B is southbound.)

DAY 2: DOWNTOWN DELIGHTS

You can spend an entire day discovering **Downtown Oranjestad's** colorful mélange of local eateries, shops, historic buildings, museums, and refurbished main street arcades and courtyards. Start at the **ArubaMade Mall** across from the cruise terminal for authentic local snacks, drinks, and island-made souvenirs (and free Wi-Fi). Then head to the area behind the beautiful pink **Royal Plaza Mall** for the free **National Museum of Archaeology,** a modern trek back through time that is worth exploring— and air-conditioned. If you really want to get the inside scoop on what makes this little

How to Spend 5 Days in Aruba

capital city tick, join a guided tour with **Aruba Walking Tours**.

To cool off, head to the urban oasis known as **Surfside Beach Bar** or the trendy seafront lounge **Reflexions**, which has its own pool. Stay for the stellar sunset, then head back to town to enjoy the lively marina region of **Renaissance Marketplace** for alfresco dining, nightlife, casinos, and free live entertainment.

LOGISTICS
Take Route 1B straight to Downtown, take a taxi, or hop a public bus.

DAY 3: GO WILD
Today's the day to explore **Arikok National Park,** the island's wild and untamed arid outback, with a guided UTV, ATV, or jeep safari with an operator like **De Palm Tours**. Don't miss the surreal thrill of swimming or snorkeling in the **Conchi,** a remote natural pool, or exploring the **Fontein Cave,** which has the island's only Arawak Indian drawings. Most tours leave on the early side, so plan to grab a quick breakfast at your hotel. If you choose a full-day affair, lunch will be included; plan dinner at your resort, as you'll be exhausted after the tour.

To explore the wild in the most eco-friendly way possible, sign up for a trek with **Aruba Nature Adventures**. If you choose to do a half-day tour, go in the morning so you can spend the afternoon at your resort's pool or at the beach before having dinner at the hotel. You'll need the downtime, trust us.

LOGISTICS
You can drive there, but it's not recommended for first-timers. All tours include hotel pickup and drop-off, so sit back and let the adventure begin.

DAY 4: SLEUTH OUT SOUTHEAST COAST SURPRISES
After a lazy morning, rent a car (or hire a private driver) for the day and head southeast to **Savaneta** for the best locally caught fish and seafood meals at **Zeerovers**. After lunch, head back to Route 1 to continue on to **San Nicolas** for its outdoor art scene; be sure to book a tour with **Aruba Murals Tours.** Don't miss a stop at **Charlie's Bar**—it's been in operation for more than 80 years—and then head to **Baby Beach** for an hour or two of beach time. Refreshments can be found at **Rum Reef,** an adult-only infinity pool and bar, or the family-friendly **Big Mama's** at the other end of the beach. Head back to Savaneta for dinner at **Flying Fishbone** or **The Old Man and the Sea,** but make sure you have a reservation well ahead for both.

LOGISTICS

For San Nicolas, follow Route 1A; for Savaneta, make a right turn at the Super S-CHOW Supermarket, and follow the sign for Flying Fishbone. Get back on 1A for San Nicolas.

DAY 5: YOUR LAST DAY

Flights usually leave in the late afternoon; spend an hour or so at the beach before heading to the airport. Make sure to leave plenty of time at the airport, as there are about seven steps that involve picking up and dropping your luggage numerous times before you clear Customs and can head to the waiting areas. The airport now has a VIP lounge, accessible if you have a Priority Pass membership or spring for the extra cost of being ushered through all the lines like a celebrity (except for U.S. customs) with **First Class Experience Aruba**.

For one last tropical cocktail, stop at "The Crying Room," a small corner of the airport's **One Happy Bar,** aptly named as it's famous for inducing the tears of those who always hate to leave Aruba. (Be forewarned: they have a sign that limits crying to 15 minutes.)

WHAT IF IT RAINS?

Even though Aruba is outside the hurricane belt, you may find yourself on a rare rainy day, or you might just want a break from the tropical heat if you overdid the sunbathing. That's a perfect time to explore some indoor attractions like the modern multilevel **Palm Beach Plaza** for all kinds of shopping and entertainment. Or check out the massive new stand-alone IMAX cinema and entertainment complex called **The Movies @ Gloria** in Eagle Beach for first-run movies, a children's play park, and lots of dining options like P.F. Chang's.

You can also enjoy some first-rate pampering at one of the island's many premium spas—maybe an aloe-based treatment to soothe your overly sunned skin or a couple's massage by the sea under a tiki hut. If you want more action, the casinos are always ready to receive you. Some are open 24 hours a day, and sometimes they offer daytime bingo.

Best Tours

Guided tours are your best option if you only have a short time, and there are many first-rate tour operators on Aruba with adventures that range from jeep safaris in the outback, to bus tours along the coast, to sea and sand discovery by boat, and even historical, art, and foodie walking tours. A good way to get your bearings is to take a bus tour of the island's main highlights—Aruba is small, so it won't take more than half a day with a well-established company like De Palm Tours. It's a great way to discover where you might like to return to later on your holiday.

Bike Tours

Aruba Motorcycle Tours

BICYCLE TOURS | Hog fans will adore this novel way to tour Aruba. On your own Harley with a rental or in one of their guided group tours—a 4-hour trip that takes only the back roads to bring you the island's best sites—you will enjoy the open road like a rebel with this outfit. A motorcycle license and $1,000 deposit is required with each tour. For rentals alone, a $2,000 deposit is required. Helmets are supplied, and pickup and drop-off at hotels is offered. All renters and group riders must be over

21. ✉ *Jaburibari 16-C, Noord* ☎ *297/641–7818* ⊕ *arubamotorcycletours.com* 🖾 *Tours from $50 (on top of rental).*

Rancho Notorious

BICYCLE TOURS | If mountain biking is more your thing, tours are offered through the Aruban countryside on old donkey trails—there are more than 200 mountain bike trails on the island—for half or full days. Bikes are TREK aluminum mountain bikes. ✉ *Boroncana, Noord* ☎ *297/699–5492* ⊕ *www.ranchonotorious.com* 🖾 *From $75.*

🚢 Boat Tours

Snorkeling and sunset party cruises are the norm, but some also include dinner on board or on shore after your voyage. Most tours depart from Palm Beach at either Pelican Pier, De Palm Pier, or the Hadicurari Pier, with a few exceptions departing from Downtown Oranjestad. There are also semi-submarine and submarine tours with Atlantis Submarines (operated by De Palm Tours), which operates a 65-foot air-conditioned sub that takes 48 passengers 95 to 130 feet below the surface along Barcadera Reef. The 2-hour trip (including boat transfer to the submarine platform and 50-minute plunge) has garnered multiple awards for best tour and one for green operations. Make reservations one day in advance. Another option is the *Seaworld Explorer*, a semisubmersible also operated by Atlantis Submarines that allows you to view Aruba's marine habitat from 6 feet below the surface.

★ De Palm Tours
SPECIAL-INTEREST TOURS | This is one of the island's largest multiservice tour companies. They offer guided tours on land and excursions at sea in a multitude of vehicle options and sea crafts, including submarines. ⊠ *L. G. Smith Blvd. 142, Oranjestad* ☎ *297/582–4400, 800/766–6016* ⊕ *depalm.com.*

Pelican Adventures
SPECIAL-INTEREST TOURS | A good selection of land and sea tours—and sometimes a combo of both—are offered by this well-established company. ⊠ *J. E. Irausquin Blvd. 237, Noord* ☎ *297/587–2302* ⊕ *www.pelican-aruba.com.*

🍴 Food Tours
★ Fusion of the World Food Tour
WALKING TOURS | Discover four different dining spots for tapas and drinks—restaurants may change, but each has an inherent connection to Aruba—all within walking distance of each

other in Downtown Oranjestad. This two-and-a-half-hour foodie tour takes place in the evening (Monday and Thursday nights only) with a local guide who will also fill you in on some history and highlights of the downtown attractions and neighborhoods you are exploring. The pace is leisurely and complimentary pickup from the major resort areas can be included, but drop-off is not. ⊠ *Cosecha Building, Zoutmanstraat 1* ✥ *Across the street from the big yellow Cosecha Building, look for the Aruba Walking Tours Meeting Point sign* ☎ *297/699–0995* ⊕ *arubawalkingtours.com/aruba-food-tour* 💰 *$89* ↺ *Max. 20 people. Adults preferred.*

★ Kukoo Kunuku Party and Foodie Tours
SPECIAL-INTEREST TOURS | Best known for their wild and crazy barhopping tours aboard brightly painted red party buses, this outfit also dials it down a notch for their foodie tours like the Dinner and Nightlife Tour that includes a sunset Champagne toast or the Wine On Down The Road Tour, which features an onboard sommelier and stops at some of Aruba's finest dining spots for wine and tapas. They also offer a happy hour tour. ⊠ *Oranjestad* ☎ *297/586–2010* ⊕ *www.kukookunuku.com* 💰 *From $59* ↺ *Adults only.*

Best Tours

 Specialty Tours

Aruba's interior is rugged and best explored with an all-terrain vehicle, especially if you want to explore the cacti-studded countryside or visit the natural pool or other landmarks like the small natural bridges or the wild coast. The island's largest tour operators like De Palm Tours and ABC Tours offer the most choices when it comes to jeep safaris and UTV tours, but if you want to go it alone, then it's best to rent a sturdy vehicle from a company that specializes in them like Off Road Evolution Aruba.

ABC Tours

ADVENTURE TOURS | FAMILY | Jeep and UTV tour itineraries include visits to Aruba's interesting historical sites, as well as natural attractions. Private curated tours also available. ☒ Schotlandstraat 61, Oranjestad ☎ 297/582-5600 ⊕ abc-aruba. com ☎ From $85.

★ Aruba Nature Adventures

SPECIAL-INTEREST TOURS | Eco-friendly exploration is the motto behind this specialty tour operator, everything they do keeps the preservation of nature at the forefront of their activities. The numerous small group outings typically have an element of health and wellness and range from yoga and meditation to in-depth information on the flora and fauna you'll encounter. The hike to the famous natural pool in Arikok National Park is the most eco-friendly and exhilarating way to experience it. ☎ 297/730–0077 ⊕ arubaeco. tours ☎ From $95.

🚶 Walking Tours

★ Aruba Walking Tours

WALKING TOURS | Explore the heartbeat of *One Happy Island* and learn all about its fascinating history on the Aruba Historic Cultural Downtown Walking Tour, which lasts about 2½ hours and covers about 30 stops, including a cooking demonstration. They also offer a foodie adventure at night called Fusions of World Food Tour which stops at five places. Complimentary pickup is included from most hotels (but not drop-off), and private and custom tours are also available.

■ TIP → **The big metal solar tree sculpture at the meeting spot has smartphone charging outlets within it. Day tour meeting time is at 9 am sharp.** ☒ Zoutmanstraat 1, Oranjestad ☎ 297/699–0995 ⊕ arubawalkingtours.com ☎ From $39 ⊗ Closed Sat., Sun. and Tues.

On the Calendar

Year-Round

Bon Bini Festival. Local music and dance festival Tuesday nights at Fort Zoutman. ⊕ *www.facebook.com/ ArubaBonBiniFestival*

Santa Rosa Farmer's Market. A large local farmers' market held the first Sunday of every month. ⊕ *www.facebook.com/ santarosa.aruba*

January—March

Carnival. Weeks of parties and cultural events precede this two-day street party in late February or early March. ⊕ *www.aruba.com/us/ calendar/aruba-carnival*

February

Carnival Grand Parade. The culmination of Carnival celebrations in Downtown Oranjestad.

March

National Flag and Anthem Day. March 18th brings celebrations to the streets. ⊕ *www.aruba. com*

April

King's Day. On April 27, Aruba celebrates Dutch King Willem-Alexander's birthday with outdoor activities.

May

Aruba Hi-Winds. An annual massive windsurfing and kiteboarding competition with parties. ⊕ *www.arubahiwinds. com*

Soul Beach Music Festival. This Memorial Day Weekend event attracts famous international music talents. ⊕ *soulbeach.net*

June

Aruba Summer Music Festival. Local and Latin American musical stars perform during the last week of June. ⊕ *www. arubasmf.com*

KLM Aruba Marathon. Marathon day also includes a half marathon, a 10K, and a 5K. ⊕ *klmarubamarathon.com*

On the Calendar

August

Aruba I Do. Every August hundreds of couples are invited to renew their vows on Eagle Beach for free. ⊕ *www.aruba.com/us/ renew-your-vows-in-aruba*

Aruba International Regatta. Three days of great boat races and parties are held in mid-August. ⊕ *aruba-regatta.org*

September

Aruba Reef Care Project Clean-Up. This island-wide event has great after-parties. ⊕ *www.facebook.com/ arubareefcarefoundation*

Aruba Art Week. San Nicolas invites international artists to permanently beautify the sunrise city during this annual event. ⊕ *arubaartfair.com*

November

Aruba Open Beach Tennis Championships. This massive international tennis competition takes place during the second week of November with plenty of parties. ⊕ *www.arubabeachtennisopen.com*

December

Dande Festival. Local musicians welcome the new year with original songs and competitions. ⊕ *www.aruba.com/us/ calendar/dande-festival*

ORANJESTAD

Updated by
Susan Campbell

👁 Sights   🍴 Restaurants   🏨 Hotels   🛍 Shopping   🍸 Nightlife

★★★☆☆   ★★★★☆   ★★☆☆☆   ★★★★☆   ★★★★☆

NEIGHBORHOOD SNAPSHOT

TOP EXPERIENCES

■ **Luxury Shopping:** Downtown's upscale shops have jewelry, watches, and brand-name fashions.

■ **Try Your Luck:** Visit glitzy world-class casinos where you can seduce Lady Luck.

■ **Walking Tours:** Explore Downtown's culture, history, and food with Aruba Walking Tours.

■ **Trolley Tour:** Take the free trolley to preview the eclectic maze of superb shopping and dining options.

■ **Surfside Beach:** Grab a bike and head out on the paved seaside trail to discover this lovely little urban beach.

GETTING HERE AND AROUND

About 15 minutes from the airport, Oranjestad is accessible by car, taxi, or public bus. The bus stops at most major resorts, as well as the Downtown terminal and all the best attractions.

PLANNING YOUR TIME

Downtown can be crowded when the cruise ships are in port; check the port authority website to see the schedule if you want to avoid the crunch. Sundays are sleepier, as many of the smaller shops close, but the main malls remain open late. Traffic can be intense at rush hours, and parking can be tricky at peak business hours (there are free lots, including the one behind the Renaissance Marketplace), but never park between yellow lines or you'll get a boot. Downtown is safe, but stick to the main streets at night.

VIEWFINDER

■ If you are seeking authentic Aruban souvenirs and food, look for the new Aruba-Made Mall just across from the cruise terminal. There are many stalls with local crafters and eats, too.

Aruba's historic port capital city Oranjestad has always had a colorful Dutch colonial charm, but the past few years have seen a major face-lift and renewal throughout Downtown to better accommodate a growing local population and better welcome the 2-million-plus visitors it sees each year.

Aruba's capital is easily explored on foot. Its palm-lined central thoroughfare runs between old and new pastel-painted buildings of typical Dutch design (Spanish influence is also evident in some of the architecture), and guided walking tours help you discover its history, culture, and food. There are a lot of malls with boutiques and shops—the Renaissance Mall carries high-end luxury items, designer fashions, and two glitzy casinos. Massive renovations continue to give Main Street (aka Caya G. F. Betico Croes), behind the Renaissance Marina Resort, a whole new lease on life with boutique malls, shops, and restaurants opening next to well-loved family-run businesses.

Pedestrian-only walkways and resting areas have unclogged the streets, and the free ecotrolley is a great way for cruise visitors to explore. Across from the cruise terminal, Local Market has locally made wares, and directly across from it, in front of the marina, you'll find the new ArubaMade Mall with locally made products, food, and drink. Further afield in the backstreets, Wilhelminastraat is fast becoming the new Downtown restaurant row, with trendy spots taking root beside legendary old establishments and exciting new venues like an artisan distillery that gives tours, tapas, and tastes.

Linear Park (an ongoing project that will connect Downtown to the main tourist beaches via sidewalks and boardwalks) begins in Oranjestad and runs all the way to the airport, providing a scenic paved path along the sea to walk, bike, or jog. It's also peppered with free public fitness equipment and it runs by urban Surfside Beach, where you'll find upscale seaside lounging and a funky beach bar side-by-side, just minutes from the Downtown core. It's also an ideal spot for plane-spotting, as they arrive right overhead.

Sights

Aruba Aloe Museum and Factory

FACTORY | Aruba has the ideal conditions to grow the aloe vera plant. It's an important export, and there are aloe stores all over the island. The museum and factory tour reveal the process of extracting the serum to make many products used for beauty, health, and healing. Free guided tours are available in English, Dutch, Spanish, and Papiamento every 15 minutes, or you can do a self-guided walking tour after their audiovisual presentation. There's a store to purchase their products on-site, but they are also available online. ∎**TIP→ Look for their reef-safe sunscreen; it's available island-wide.** ⊠ *Pitastraat 115, Oranjestad* ☎ *297/588–3222* ⊕ *arubaaloe.com* ⊠ *Free.*

Cas Di Cultura

ARTS CENTER | The National Theater of Aruba, the island's cultural center, hosts art exhibits, folkloric shows, dance performances, and concerts throughout the year. ⊠ *Stichting Shouwburg Aruba, Vondellaan 2, Oranjestad* ☎ *297/582–1010* ⊕ *casdicultura.aw.*

★ De Palm Private Island

ISLAND | **FAMILY** | This delightful private island experience encompasses all ages, even toddlers, but it has numerous adult-oriented enclaves with premium seating, beach cabanas, and big luxe cabana rentals with VIP service and private bars. They also have their own flock of flamingos in a protected area. All-inclusive packages include all food and drink, access to a colorful kids' waterpark, adult body-drop waterslides, banana boat rides, snorkel equipment, guided snorkel tours, and fun activities like salsa lessons. Additional add-ons include their signature Seatrek experience, an underwater air helmet walk, as well as SNUBA deep-dive snorkeling, and spa services. The water taxi to the island is free, and hotel pickup and drop-off options are available. The island is completely accessible, including the water taxi, and they offer a complimentary amphibious wheelchair. ∎**TIP→ The reef is home to huge neon blue ever-smiling parrotfish, so bring an underwater camera!** ⊠ *De Palm Island Ferry Terminal, De Palm Island Way Z/N, Oranjestad* ☎ *297/522–4400* ⊕ *depalmisland.com* ⊠ *From $115, including bus; from $109, no bus.*

Fort Zoutman

MILITARY SIGHT | One of the island's oldest edifices, Aruba's historic fort was built in 1796 and played an important role in skirmishes between British and Curaçao troops in 1803. The Willem III Tower, named for the Dutch monarch of that time, was added in 1868 to serve as a lighthouse. Over time the fort has been a government

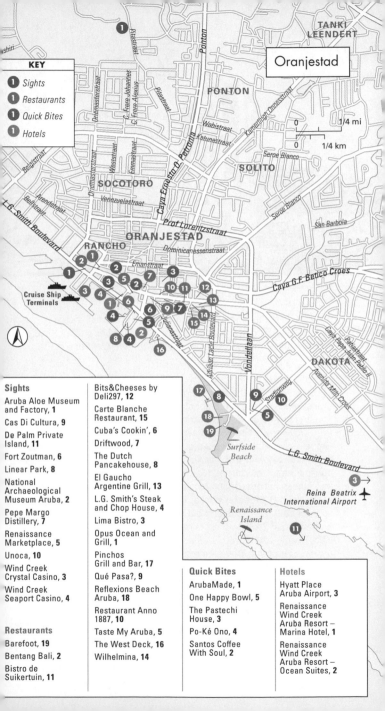

Oranjestad

KEY
- **1** Sights
- **1** Restaurants
- **1** Quick Bites
- **1** Hotels

Cruise Ship Terminals

Surfside Beach

Renaissance Island

Reina Beatrix International Airport

Sights

Aruba Aloe Museum and Factory, **1**

Cas Di Cultura, **9**

De Palm Private Island, **11**

Fort Zoutman, **6**

Linear Park, **8**

National Archaeological Museum Aruba, **2**

Pepe Margo Distillery, **7**

Renaissance Marketplace, **5**

Unoca, **10**

Wind Creek Crystal Casino, **3**

Wind Creek Seaport Casino, **4**

Restaurants

Barefoot, **19**

Bentang Bali, **2**

Bistro de Suikertuin, **11**

Bits&Cheeses by Deli297, **12**

Carte Blanche Restaurant, **15**

Cuba's Cookin', **6**

Driftwood, **7**

The Dutch Pancakehouse, **8**

El Gaucho Argentine Grill, **13**

L.G. Smith's Steak and Chop House, **4**

Lima Bistro, **3**

Opus Ocean and Grill, **1**

Pinchos Grill and Bar, **17**

Qué Pasa?, **9**

Reflexions Beach Aruba, **18**

Restaurant Anno 1887, **10**

Taste My Aruba, **5**

The West Deck, **16**

Wilhelmina, **14**

Quick Bites

ArubaMade, **1**

One Happy Bowl, **5**

The Pastechi House, **3**

Po-Ké Ono, **4**

Santos Coffee With Soul, **2**

Hotels

Hyatt Place Aruba Airport, **3**

Renaissance Wind Creek Aruba Resort – Marina Hotel, **1**

Renaissance Wind Creek Aruba Resort – Ocean Suites, **2**

Built in 1798 by the Dutch army, Fort Zoutman is Aruba's oldest structure.

office building, a police station, a prison, and a small museum (now closed). The courtyard is where the weekly Bon Bini ("welcome") Festival takes place. ⊠ *Zoutmanstraat, Oranjestad.*

★ Linear Park

CITY PARK | FAMILY | Plaza Turismo, off Surfside Beach, is the anchor of Linear Park which, when completed, will connect both main tourist beaches along the coast by boardwalks and walking paths. The first leg—a smooth paved biking and jogging trail that runs from Downtown Oranjestad along the sea all the way to the airport—is complete. There are many cafés, bars, and snack stops along the way, and there are also fitness pit stops with free-to-use public fitness equipment. It's a popular stretch for local fun runs and fitness initiatives, and locals and visitors use the easy-to-access Green Bike rental kiosks. The plaza has also become a go-to spot for cultural events and outdoor entertainment. A new portion was added in 2021 to the Malmok area that ends at Fisherman's Huts Beach. Both stretches have become popular treks for electric scooter riders; there are many new app-operated rental spots. When complete, Linear Park will be the longest of its kind in the entire Caribbean. ⊠ *Surfside Beach and Malmok, Oranjestad* 🖃 *Free.*

★ National Archaeological Museum Aruba

HISTORY MUSEUM | Walking around Downtown Oranjestad, look for a blue ceramic horse and an ancient canoe out front of a massive mustard-yellow and olive-green complex. This beautifully restored heritage home was once owned by the Ecury family and it's since been transformed into an ultra-modern, air-conditioned museum with interactive exhibits showcasing over 5,000 years of Amerindian culture. More than 10,000 artifacts are on display, and special exhibits by local artists are hosted on a regular basis. ■TIP→ For cruise visitors, it's a short walk behind the Royal Plaza Mall if you get off at that trolley stop. It's also a stop on Aruba Walking Tours. ⊠ Schelpstraat 42, Oranjestad ☎ 297/582–8979 ⊕ www.facebook. com/namaruba ⛴ Free ⊗ Closed weekends.

Pepe Margo Distillery

DISTILLERY | Housed in a recently restored historic home, this new boutique artisanal distillery in Downtown Oranjestad is producing some unique island spirits like their Nautical Rum. Tours of their facility and tastings are available. ⊠ Wilhelminastraat 46, Oranjestad ⊕ pepemargodistillery.com ⊗ Closed Sun.

Renaissance Marketplace

STORE/MALL | **FAMILY** | The complex beside the Oranjestad marina and the park around it is the place where you're most likely to happen upon some great free entertainment, including pop-up festivals. Although there's live entertainment every night at the far end in the common area bandstand, many of the bars and cafés also have their own music. You'll also find a casino, movie theaters, and arty little shops that are open late. Occasionally, there's a big gala music festival, and every Friday night there's a local artisans' market from 7–10 pm. Even if there's no planned additional activity, it's a wonderful spot to explore in the evening to experience a truly enchanting tropical night full of colorful lights and sounds along the water. ■TIP→ Look for the statue of giant flamingos to find it. ⊠ L. G. Smith Blvd. 9, Oranjestad ☎ 297/523–6065 ⊕ www.themarketplacearuba.com ⛴ Free.

UNOCA

ARTS CENTER | Although UNOCA is Aruba's national gallery, it's much more, acting as an anchor to host cultural and performance events. ⊠ Stadionweg 21, Oranjestad ☎ 297/583–5681 ⊕ unoca. aw.

CASINOS

Wind Creek Crystal Casino

CASINO | Part of the Renaissance Aruba Wind Creek Resort, this glittering casino evokes Monaco's grand establishments. There are lots of modern slots, table games like blackjack, roulette, Baccarat, and different types of poker. This casino is popular among cruise-ship passengers, who stroll over from the port to watch and play in tournaments and bet on sporting events. Open 24 hours a day, 7 days a week, it's a great place for late-night bites and drinks, which are served in the lounge until 6 am.

Did You Know?

There are eight blue horse statues located around Oranjestad's Downtown; this one is in front of the cotton-candy-colored Royal Plaza Mall. These sculptures are a reminder of Aruba's important relationship with horses.

✉ *Renaissance Wind Creek Aruba Resort, L. G. Smith Blvd. 82, Oranjestad* ☎ *297/583–6000* ⊕ *windcreek.com/aruba.*

★ Wind Creek Seaport Casino

CASINO | This super-lively casino right on the waterfront, across the street from the Renaissance Marketplace, is open until 4 am. With more than 300 modern slots, four blackjack tables, Caribbean stud, roulette, and regular poker, there are also state-of-the-art race and sports book operations. **■TIP→ The casino is behind the giant flamingo statues.** ✉ *L. G. Smith Blvd. 9, Oranjestad* ☎ *297/583–6000 ext. 6318* ⊕ *windcreek.com/aruba.*

Beaches

Renaissance Island

BEACH | FAMILY | This 40-acre tropical oasis is accessible only to guests of the Renaissance Wind Creek Aruba Resort unless you buy a day pass (which are only available when resorts are not at full capacity.) Free boat shuttles pick up non-resort guests in the lower lobby of the marina resort. Iguana Beach is family-friendly, while Flamingo Beach is limited to adults and hosts half a dozen resident flamingos. (Children may visit the flamingos for a photo op daily from 9–10 am but must have an adult present.) The waters are clear and full of colorful fish; swimming/snorkeling is in a protected area, and there's a full-service restaurant, beach bars, and waiter service on the beach. Rent a full-service cabana for more luxuries. Nonguests can book a treatment at their Okeanos Spa and gain access to the island afterward for free. Go early to snag a cool overwater hammock. **Amenities:** food and drink; toilets; showers; water sports. **Best for:** swimming; snorkeling. ✉ *Oranjestad* ✛ *Accessible by water taxi only from the Renaissance Wind Creek Aruba Resort and Marina* ☎ *297/583–6000* ⊕ *www.marriott.com/en-us/hotels/auabr-renaissance-wind-creek-aruba-resort/renaissance-island/* ▣ *Day pass $125 includes lunch and drink.*

Surfside Beach

BEACH | FAMILY | Right behind Plaza Turismo and accessible by public bus, car, or taxi, this little urban beach just outside Downtown Oranjestad has two distinctly different beach bars, one for casual surf-side fun and the other more upscale, with its own pool and high-end food and drink that's open for breakfast, lunch, and dinner. It's easily accessible via the paved Linear Park as well, making it an ideal spot to stop for a dip when cycling or jogging along the bike path or strolling around the town. Plane-spotting is a given, since it's only 2 minutes from the airport. **Amenities:** food and drink; parking (free); toilets; water sports. **Best for:** swimming;

partiers; sunset. ⊠ *L. G. Smith Blvd., Oranjestad* ⚓ *Just before the airport compound* ⊕ *www.aruba.com/us/explore/ surfside-beach.*

🍴 Restaurants

★ Barefoot
$$$$ | CONTEMPORARY | One of Aruba's most popular toes-in-the-sand spots (even their indoor dining has sand on the floor), it's all about creative international fusion cuisine, comprehensive upscale wine choices, and superb signature cocktails in an ultimate barefoot-luxury setting. The sunset views are always spectacular. **Known for:** romantic toes-in-the-sand dining; creative fusions like lobster-cappuccino bisque; great service and consistent quality fare. ⑤ *Average main: $35* ⊠ *L. G. Smith Blvd. 1, Oranjestad* ⚓ *on Surfside Beach* ☎ *297/588–9824* ⊕ *barefootaruba.com* ⊘ *No lunch.*

Bentang Bali
$$ | INDONESIAN | The Dutch still have strong culinary ties to Indonesia, so this welcome addition to Downtown offers an ideal place to indulge in quality comfort food from that corner of the globe. Exotic and traditional Asian specialties also abound, and this is one of the few places on the island where you can sample the elusive *rijsttafel* (rice table), a large assortment of small dishes meant to be shared by a group. **Known for:** homemade black pasta and dumplings; large selection of vegetarian and vegan dishes; an eclectic selection of seafood, like king crab and calamari. ⑤ *Average main: $15* ⊠ *Havenstraat 36 B, Oranjestad* ☎ *297/280–0440* ⊕ *bentangbalirestaurant.com* ⊘ *Closed Mon.*

★ Bistro De Suikertuin
$$ | INTERNATIONAL | This charming bistro dining spot is the quintessential meeting place for those seeking great signature cocktails, creative tapas, quality coffee, and healthy lunch options. They also offer a full dinner menu, with dishes that range from chicken cordon bleu to beef tenderloin with Dutch potatoes. **Known for:** elegant royal high tea and high wine services; Aruban and Indonesian dishes like *keshi yena* and *nasi goreng*; lovely shaded courtyard with big tables for group socializing. ⑤ *Average main: $20* ⊠ *Wilhelminastraat 64, Oranjestad* ☎ *297/582–6322* ⊕ *www. desuikertuin.com* ⊘ *Closed Sun.*

★ Bits&Cheeses by Deli297

$$ | **INTERNATIONAL** | What began as a catering company became so popular that they decided to open a brick-and-mortar café in the heart of Downtown Oranjestad, so now you can dine inside their cheery space to enjoy breakfast, lunch, and dinner with an amazing selection of gourmet cheeses, quality charcuterie, and a surprising selection of fine wines, too. Grab one of their BC boxes to go for a perfect picnic, or a lavish platter of goodies to entertain guests back at your hotel. **Known for:** quality catering and delivery of gourmet fare; special baskets and boards of meats and cheeses; creative paninis and pastas. $ *Average main: $20* ⊠ *Wilhelminastraat 63, Oranjestad* ☎ *297/566–5264* ⊕ *www.facebook.com/ bitsandcheeses* ⊗ *Closed Sun. and Mon.*

Carte Blanche Restaurant

$$$$ | **ECLECTIC** | Created by Chef Dennis van Daatselaar, this intimate chef's table experience for 14 people is set in a tropical garden. Come with an open-minded and expect the unexpected as tasting new experiences is the focus here, and though every dish might not be to your individual taste, the overall adventure is typically well applauded by visiting foodies. **Known for:** consistently creative quality cuisine; an impressive wine list; an enjoyable culinary adventure. $ *Average main: $109* ⊠ *Wilhelminastraat 74, Oranjestad* ☎ *297/586–3339* ⊕ *www.carteblanchearuba.com* ⊗ *Closed Sun and Mon. No lunch.*

★ Cuba's Cookin'

$$$ | **CUBAN** | This red-hot landmark establishment in the heart of Renaissance Marketplace specializes in traditional Havana specialties and is the only spot on Aruba where you can enjoy an authentic Cuban sandwich for lunch. There's even a surprisingly good selection of gluten-free, vegetarian, and vegan fare on offer. **Known for:** melt-in-your-mouth ropa vieja (Cuba's national skirt steak dish); hot live music and alfresco dancing seven nights a week; an impressive selection of original Cuban art. $ *Average main: $28* ⊠ *Renaissance Marketplace, L. G. Smith Blvd. 82, Oranjestad* ☎ *297/588–0627* ⊕ *cubascookin.com.*

Driftwood

$$$ | **CARIBBEAN** | **FAMILY** | Opened in 1986, this rustic nautical-themed restaurant is owned and operated by the Merryweather family. It's justifiably famous for serving up the freshest catch of the day caught by the owners themselves. **Known for:** family-recipe hearty fish soup; boat-to-table fresh fish and other seafood; friendly service and warm atmosphere. $ *Average main: $30* ⊠ *Klipstraat 12, Oranjestad* ☎ *297/583–2515* ⊕ *www.driftwoodaruba.com* ⊗ *Closed Sun.*

Most Aruba restaurants are casual and fun places for a drink and a meal.

★ The Dutch Pancakehouse

$$ | DUTCH | FAMILY | Dutch pancakes are unlike North American-style flapjacks since they can be both savory and sweet, offering opportunities for breakfast, lunch, and dinner, and this legendary spot in the Renaissance Marketplace is considered the absolute best place to try them. More like thin crepes, they can be covered in (or stuffed with) a multitude of ingredients, which might include meats, vegetables, and cheeses. **Known for:** over 50 styles of sweet and savory Dutch-style pancakes; a surprising selection of excellent schnitzels; consistently good-quality fare and friendly service. $ *Average main: $15 ⊠ Renaissance Marketplace, L. G. Smith Blvd. 9, Oranjestad* ☎ *297/583–7180* ⊕ *www.thedutchpancakehouse.com.*

El Gaucho Argentine Grill

$$$$ | STEAKHOUSE | FAMILY | Aruba's original go-to for carnivores since 1977, El Gaucho is famous for meat served in mammoth portions. Though to be honest, it's not all about meat; seafood platters are something to consider as well. **Known for:** 16-ounce Gaucho steak; largest shish kebab on the island; strolling musicians who create a fun and boisterous atmosphere. $ *Average main: $40 ⊠ Wilhelminastraat 80, Oranjestad* ☎ *297/582–3677* ⊕ *www.elgaucho-aruba.com* ☾ *Closed Sun.*

L. G. Smith's Steak and Chop House

$$$$ | STEAKHOUSE | A study in teak, cream, and black, this fine steak house offers some of the best beef on the island. Subdued lighting and cascading water create an elegant atmosphere, and the view over the harbor makes for an exceptional dining experience. **Known for:** USDA-certified Angus beef; excellent wine list and stellar signature cocktails; four-course beef and wine tasting menu from around the world. ⑤ *Average main: $50* ⊠ *Renaissance Wind Creek Aruba Resort and Casino, L. G. Smith Blvd. 82, Oranjestad* ☎ *297/523–6195* ⊕ *www.lgsmiths.com* ☯ *No lunch.*

Lima Bistro

$$$ | PERUVIAN | Considering its secret location in the bottom corner of Harbour House, this adorable little Peruvian-themed escape has garnered a big buzz for its food, likely because owner Chef Teddy Bouroncle is well-known for his culinary talents from his tenure at the Aruba Marriott. Dine inside or out and enjoy traditional Peruvian dishes like *lomo saltado* or their special take on ceviche. **Known for:** creative takes on traditional Peruvian fare; elevated street food and killer authentic cocktails; warm and inviting family-run atmosphere. ⑤ *Average main: $25* ⊠ *Harbour House, Weststraat 2, Oranjestad* ☎ *297/741–2705* ⊕ *www.limabistro.com* ☯ *Closed Sun. No lunch.*

Opus Ocean and Grill

$$$ | INTERNATIONAL | Mauve mood lighting and enchanting fairy lights set the stage for this intimate little family-run restaurant specializing in seafood and grilled meats. The menu is not comprehensive, but what they do very well includes beautifully prepared shrimp and grilled-to-perfection tomahawk steaks. **Known for:** excellent homemade fish soup; attentive and knowledgeable service; rotating chef's specials, like paella and seafood pasta. ⑤ *Average main: $25* ⊠ *Havenstraat 36 B, Oranjestad* ☎ *297/280–0120* ⊕ *opusaruba.com* ☯ *No lunch.*

★ Pinchos Grill and Bar

$$$$ | ECLECTIC | One of the most romantic settings on the island is highlighted by enchanting twinkling lights strung over the water on a pier. *Pinchos* ("skewers" in Spanish) offers a fairly extensive menu of both meat and seafood skewers in addition to more creative main courses. **Known for:** romantic pier-side atmosphere; signature sangria; excellent personalized service. ⑤ *Average main: $35* ⊠ *L. G. Smith Blvd. 7, Oranjestad* ☎ *297/583–2666* ⊕ *www.pinchosaruba.com* ☯ *No lunch.*

Qué Pasa?

$$$ | **ECLECTIC** | Despite the name, the fare here is not Mexican but much more international with some real surprises, like a comprehensive sushi menu. The staff is helpful and friendly, creative chef specials change often, and it's a great spot to stop in for signature cocktails and special tapas; don't miss their a la carte weekend brunches or their Grand Dessert, four chef-special treats on one plate. **Known for:** early bird menu weekdays 4–6 pm; an eclectic assortment of international dishes; all-you-can-eat sushi on Wednesday. $ *Average main: $30* ⊠ *Wilhelminastraat 18, Oranjestad* ☎ *297/583–4888* ⊕ *www.quepasaaruba.com* ☉ *No lunch Mon.–Thurs.*

Reflexions Beach Aruba

$$$ | **INTERNATIONAL** | A sophisticated upscale spot on the water minutes from Downtown Oranjestad does its best to replicate the South Beach Miami scene with luxe cabanas, daybeds, and beach and pool service around a chic seaside bar. Dinner is mostly laid-back in high style with a good selection of quality cuts of meats and fresh fish and seafood, plus a good selection of fine Champagnes. **Known for:** happy hours with live music; great pool right on the beach; stunning sunsets and chic vibe. $ *Average main: $25* ⊠ *L. G. Smith Blvd. 1D, Surfside Beach, Oranjestad* ☎ *297/582–0153* ⊕ *www.reflexionsaruba.com.*

Restaurant Anno 1887

$$$ | **FRENCH** | Those still mourning the loss of two of Aruba's most beloved old dining spots—Chez Mathilde and Le Dome—can dry their eyes, because some of the original players of those establishments have teamed up to create the same type of classic French experience in Downtown Oranjestad. Expect impeccable personal service and classic French fare like *tournedos au poivre* (beef in red wine) and coq au vin, but vegan options can also be requested on site. **Known for:** French dishes like bouillabaisse de Marseille and chocolate or Grand Marnier soufflé; quality ingredients always prepared "a la minute"; prix-fixe five-course chef tasting menu. $ *Average main: $30* ⊠ *Wilheminastraat 27, Oranjestad* ☎ *297/583–0020* ⊕ *www.restaurantanno1877.com* ☉ *Closed Sun. No lunch.*

Surfside Beach Bar

$$ | **INTERNATIONAL** | **FAMILY** | Enjoy cool and creative cocktails and beach shack eats in the afternoon on a pristine stretch of white sand and aqua sea, just minutes from Downtown Oranjestad. The fun and friendly vibe includes beach service, lounge and umbrella rentals, and happy hour drink specials. **Known for:** Sunday barbecue noon–7 pm; casual fare like burgers, spicy shrimp, fish and

chips, and create-your-own pizzas; hearty Dutch-style breakfasts Friday–Sunday. [S] *Average main: $12* ⊠ *Surfside Beach, Oranjestad* ☎ *297/280–6584* ⊕ *www.surfsidearuba.com.*

★ Taste My Aruba

$$$$ | CARIBBEAN | Foodies in the know are beating a path to this down-to-earth eatery housed in a beautifully restored 100-year-old heritage house to enjoy locally sourced fare, especially fresh fish and local lobster. The menu changes daily depending on the bounty but rarely disappoints, with the driving force of repeat business due to the larger-than-life personality of owner Nathaly de Mey and the culinary skills of her top-notch chefs and creative mixologists. **Known for:** expertly prepared fresh fish straight from the boat; authentic local experience and locally sourced fare; outstanding personal service and welcoming atmosphere. [S] *Average main: $32* ⊠ *Wilhelminastraat 57, Oranjestad* ☎ *297/588–1600* ⊕ *tastemyaruba.com* ⊗ *Closed Sun.*

The West Deck

$$ | CARIBBEAN | FAMILY | Opened by the same people who own Pinchos, this fun and friendly wood-decked grill joint offers casual fare like barbecue ribs and grilled shrimp by the dozen, as well as Caribbean bites like jerk wings, fried *funchi* (like a thick polenta) with Dutch cheese, and West Indian samosas. There are some surprisingly snazzy main dishes, and the signature "Beer-Ritas" (a full bottle of beer served upside down in a big margarita) are legendary. **Known for:** a great pit stop along Linear Park; eclectic selection of Caribbean fare; superb sunset views on Surfside Beach. [S] *Average main: $20* ⊠ *L. G. Smith Blvd. at Governor's Bay Beach, Oranjestad* ☎ *297/587–2667* ⊕ *www.thewestdeck.com.*

Wilhelmina

$$$$ | INTERNATIONAL | Choose from a simple and elegant indoor dining area or a tropical outdoor garden oasis as you sample a creative international menu that includes choices of quality meats, homemade pastas, and fresh fish and seafood, all with suggested wine pairings from the well-regarded cellar. The menu also includes an impressive offering of avant-garde vegetarian dishes. **Known for:** creative takes on conventional dishes, like a signature salad with rock lobster and scallops; excellent selection of fine wines; exotic mains like Surinamese sea bass and Indonesian-style roast pork. [S] *Average main: $40* ⊠ *Wilhelmenastraat 74, Oranjestad* ☎ *297/583–0445* ⊕ *www.wilhelminaaruba.com* ⊗ *Closed Mon. No lunch.*

Offering free Wi-Fi, ArubaMade is a great place to stop for local food and souvenirs.

 Coffee and Quick Bites

ArubaMade

$ | INTERNATIONAL | Look for the beautiful bird mural across from the marina for excellent authentic Aruban-made bits and bites, including island-roasted coffee, Johnny cakes, little silver-dollar-sized Dutch pancakes, homemade ice cream, fresh coconut juice, and more. There's also an alfresco bar with full-size local-fare meals, but remember to bring cash as not all kiosks take cards. **Known for:** free Wi-Fi and lots of indoor and outdoor seating; local artisans selling locally made souvenirs; all products and fare authentic Aruban. ⑤ *Average main: $8* ⊠ *L. G. Smith Blvd. 100, Oranjestad* ☎ *297/699–1001* ⊘ *Closed Sun.*

★ Coffee Break

$ | INTERNATIONAL | Enjoy locally roasted coffee at this cheery spot and take home some of their special Aruba blend as an ideal souvenir. They also offer gelato, locally made pastries, soups, and sandwiches. **Known for:** barista-style concoctions; their own Aruba blend with coconut; fresh modern air-conditioned pit stop. ⑤ *Average main: $10* ⊠ *Caya G. F. Betico Croes 101-A, Oranjestad* ☎ *297/588–5569* Ⓜ *Downtown Trolley line.*

★ One Happy Bowl

$$ | VEGETARIAN | You need not be a vegan or seeking gluten-free options to thoroughly enjoy the creative takes on strictly plant-based fare at this happy little nook, but if you are, it's bound to be your new paradise. It's tiny though, so if you intend to dine in, reservations are a must, though there is a bustling takeout and delivery business, too. **Known for:** create your own plant-based poke bowls; all-day breakfast specials; vegan high tea first Sunday of every month. $ *Average main: $13* ✉ *Cas di Cultura, Vondellaan 2, Oranjestad* ☎ *297/641–8919 WhatsApp* ⊕ *onehappybowl.com* ◷ *No dinner.*

The Pastechi House

$ | **CARIBBEAN** | **FAMILY** | Look for the big smiling *pastechi* sign and a line of locals waiting to grab Aruba's favorite fast food (think empanada). Order one for yourself and wash it down with a cold *batido* (fruit shake). **Known for:** largest selection of pastechi types; vegan options also available; popular local pit stop. $ *Average main: $10* ✉ *Caya G. F. Betico Croes 42, Oranjestad* ⊕ *www.facebook.com/thepastechihouse* ▤ *No credit cards* ◷ *Closed Sun.* ☞ *Cash only* Ⓜ *Downtown Trolley line.*

★ Po-Ké Ono

$$ | **ASIAN** | The second location of Chef Urvin Croes' poke, bao, and sushi spot is an ideal place to watch the boats in the marina and enjoy an awesome alfresco lunch, dinner, or post-shopping or pre-casino snack. The award-winning chef is known island-wide for his artistic plating and modern cooking at his upscale outfit called Infini, but this franchise shows off his playful side with fun creative tweaks on fusion Asian cuisine and comfort food. **Known for:** top quality creative fare; killer good tiki cocktails; appealing colorful plating. $ *Average main: $15* ✉ *Renaissance Marketplace, L. G. Smith Blvd 9, Unit 25, Oranjestad* ☎ *297/280–0774* ⊕ *poke-onoaruba.com.*

★ Santos Coffee with Soul

$ | **CAFÉ** | The Eagle Beach location of this café was so popular because of its excellent coffee, creative snacks, and master baristas that they opened this Downtown location. They are also licensed for cocktails, wine, and beer and make decadent milkshakes, too. **Known for:** all day breakfast sandwiches with a twist; surprises like vegan pancake or chocolate fondue; happy hours with special fare. $ *Average main: $8* ✉ *Zoutmanstraat 7, Oranjestad* ⊹ *Across from the old fort* ☎ *287/280–8070* ⊕ *santos-aruba.com.*

Hotels

Hyatt Place Aruba Airport

$ | HOTEL | Connected directly to the airport by a covered walkway, this contemporary hotel serves the needs of business and leisure travelers on a budget and is especially convenient for those with flight cancellations. **Pros:** lovely outdoor pool with bar service; sofa beds in every room make for flexible accommodations; free shuttle to Downtown and two beaches. **Cons:** no balconies in any of the rooms; not on the beach; little to do within walking distance. ⑤ *Rooms from: $213* ✉ *Aruba Airport, Wayaca 6B, Oranjestad* ☎ *297/523–1234* ⊕ *www.hyatt.com/en-US/hotel/aruba/hyatt-place-aruba-airport/auaza* ➲ *116 rooms* ❖| *Free Breakfast.*

Renaissance Wind Creek Aruba Resort – Marina Hotel

$$$ | HOTEL | The adults-only hotel of the Renaissance Wind Creek's twin resorts offers guests a chic, waterfront urban oasis overlooking the Downtown marina with fine dining, a cool club infinity bar, and a glitzy on-site casino. **Pros:** in the heart of the best Downtown shopping and dining; good choice of in-hotel nightlife and restaurants and in-house casino; beautiful private island beach with deluxe cabana rentals. **Cons:** rooms are small and have no balconies; marina pool is tiny; water taxis are not accessible for those with mobility issues. ⑤ *Rooms from: $464* ✉ *Renaissance Beach, L. G. Smith Blvd. 82, Oranjestad* ☎ *297/583–6000, 800/421–8188* ⊕ *www.marriott.com/en-us/hotels/auabr-renaissance-wind-creek-aruba-resort/overview/* ➲ *296 rooms* ❖| *No Meals.*

Renaissance Wind Creek Aruba Resort – Ocean Suites

$$$$ | RESORT | FAMILY | Completely renovated in 2022, the family-friendly option of the Renaissance Wind Creek's twin resorts offers modern spacious suites with two pools and its own man-made beach in the heart of Oranjestad. **Pros:** small kitchenettes are convenient for families; spacious balconies; steps from Downtown attractions. **Cons:** limited dining on-site; limited water sports; water taxis are not accessible for those with mobility issues. ⑤ *Rooms from: $543* ✉ *Renaissance Beach, L. G. Smith Blvd. 82, Oranjestad* ☎ *297/583–6000* ⊕ *www.marriott.com/en-us/hotels/auabr-renaissance-wind-creek-aruba-resort/overview/* ➲ *259 rooms* ❖| *No Meals.*

Brewing Up Something Special

Order a "Balashi cocktail" in Aruba only if you want to receive a glass of water. That's because the water purification plant is in Balashi. And don't be afraid to drink the water: it's safe, delicious, and made from desalinated seawater. But since the advent of the beer called Balashi—the only beer in the world made from desalinated seawater—you might confuse a barkeep if you order just a "Balashi." Try a Balashi Chill with a wedge of lime in the neck, like many Mexican beers. Keep an eye out for their limited edition brews, too, like Magic Mango; they rotate in new ones on a regular basis.

Nightlife

Businesses come and go in the alfresco Renaissance Marketplace on the marina, but it's always lively in the evenings when most of the cafés, bistros, and restaurants transform their vibe with their own live music or entertainment. The sparkling lights on the water and the live bands playing in the common square every evening also add to the magic. This popular gathering spot is also the place where you'll find evening pop-up festivals, and there are special events from businesses like Cuba's Cookin and Café the Plaza.

Sleuth out mixologist masters at secret spots like Apotek Speakeasy, and though it's not a bar, the landmark snack spot Djiespie's Place in the back streets of Downtown is worth a mention for its outdoor dance party with live music provided by legendary old local bands every Friday night at 6 pm. It's an authentic Aruban night out, and visitors are welcome to join in.

For trendy nightlife there's Blue at the Renaissance Wind Creek Resort, and the Downtown casinos are open until the wee hours.

BARS
★ Alfie's in Aruba
PUBS | Owned by a lively expat Canadian couple, this popular watering hole in the back streets of Downtown has been attracting people from all over the world to sample their hospitality and over 50 types of craft beer. Live music Thursday, Friday, and Saturday nights also attracts the crowds, and their pub food is to die for. Think seven-cheese mac 'n' cheese nights, crispy Nashville-style fried chicken with a kick, melt-in-your-mouth ribs, and mega-burgers so big you can hardly fit them in your mouth. But they haven't forgotten their homeland; authentic Quebec-style

poutine and even vegan poutine are also both available there. Look for the big Canadian flag out front. ⊠ *Dominicanessen-straat 10, Oranjestad* ☎ *297/568–5440* ⊕ *www.alfiesinaruba.com* ☽ *Closed Sun. and Mon. No lunch* ☞ *Reservations recommended for a table between 6 and 8:30 pm.*

★ Amante Tapas Aruba

COCKTAIL LOUNGES | Under the same roof as Taste My Aruba but with a separate entrance, you'll find this clandestine little spot named after the Spanish term for "lover" as the ideal canoodling spot for you and your significant other. It's all about sharing and pairing food and drink with an ever-changing menu of interna-tionally inspired tapas and craft cocktails specifically designed to enhance each dish. The vibe is bordello sexy, with low lighting to entice you to share your innermost secrets while you feed each other sensory delights. There's also a full bar and often soft live flamenco music. Open until midnight on weekends and 11 pm weekdays. ⊠ *Wilhelminastraat 57, Oranjestad* ☎ *297/588–1600* ⊕ *amantetapasaruba.com* ☽ *Closed Sun. and Mon.* ☞ *Reserva-tions essential.*

Apotek Speakeasy

COCKTAIL LOUNGES | It's no longer a well-kept secret that Aruba has a Prohibition-style speakeasy, and discerning drinkers are flocking to this Downtown hideaway. Themed like an old-fashioned apoth-ecary—promising to handcraft potent libations to cure whatever ails you—their dedicated barkeeps are more chemists and mix-ologists than drink slingers, and they really put on a show while using carefully curated ingredients to create complicated libations that impress. The place is tiny, so reservations are a must, but it is well worth the extra effort if you're a true cocktail connoisseur. Curated private experiences can also be reserved like "A Night with Cupid" or "Sip and Savor Pairings" on different nights of the week. ⊠ *Klipstraat 2, Oranjestad* ☎ *297/561–1563* ⊕ *apotekspeak-easy.com* ☽ *Closed Sun. and Mon.*

★ BLUE

LIVE MUSIC | Located steps away from the cool infinity pool of the Renaissance Wind Creek Resort Marina Hotel, BLUE is one of the hippest social gathering spots on the island. It's the place where young local professionals gather for happy hour during the week. Later it morphs into a hot, nightly DJ-driven scene bathed in blue and violet lights with a giant video wall and talented barkeeps serving upscale concoctions like their signature BLUE Solo Mar-tini. ⊠ *Renaissance Wind Creek Resort Marina Hotel, L. G. Smith Blvd. 82, Oranjestad* ☎ *297/583–6000* ⊕ *www.marriott.com.*

Eet-Café The Paddock

BARS | It's impossible to miss the big red roof just off the marina, especially since there is a large Holstein cow on top of it! But that's the point. Wild, crazy, and whimsical is their claim to fame, and there's no better spot in town to catch Dutch *futball* if you're seeking the craziest orange-clad die-hard fans. Though it's a popular tourist lunch spot during the day, this joint really morphs into party-hearty mode at night, full of carousing locals and visitors alike enjoying the great deals on drinks via the late-night happy hours and dollar-beer specials. There are great views of the marina from the outdoor terrace. ⊠ *L. G. Smith Blvd. 13, Oranjestad* ☎ *297/583–2334* ⊕ *www.facebook.com/thepaddockaruba.*

5 o'Clock Somewhere Bar and Grill

BARS | Though this massive circular alfresco bar in the middle of Renaissance Marketplace might resemble Jimmy Buffet's Margaritaville, it's not part of the franchise—though it certainly evokes the same vibe with two daily happy hours. Think large frozen tropical cocktails, island music, and typical beach-bar fare like wings, tacos, and burgers. Surprisingly, it's also a great spot to try some locally inspired fare like snack platters of pastechi and Dutch *krokets* and individual portions of *keshi yena*, which is considered Aruba's national dish. ⊠ *Renaissance Marketplace, L. G. Smith Blvd. 82, Oranjestad* ☎ *297/523–6782* ⊕ *www.facebook. com/5somewherearuba.*

★ Hoya Cocktail Bar

COCKTAIL LOUNGES | This sophisticated alfresco emporium has totally transformed the courtyard of Plaza Daniel Leo into an exciting gathering spot, offering up cool tapas like Argentinian artisanal empanadas and a large selection of killer creative handcrafted cocktails and sangrias. It's also a champagne and wine bar. There's a cheery tropical vibe, and beyond the bar and tables there are also oversized lounging swings if you want to imbibe in style. Daily happy hour is 4–6 pm with great music. ⊠ *Plaza Daniel Leo, Oranjestad* ☎ *297/562–3515* ⊕ *hoyalush.com.*

Lucy's Retired Surfers Bar and Restaurant

BARS | It may not be on the beach, but Lucy's has the quintessential beach bar vibe; there is even a small man-made beach area outside replete with hammocks. By day it's a lunch spot serving up burgers and hearty American fare, but it ramps up the vibe at happy hour with live music and creative drink specials until just after sundown. All-day Taco Tuesdays draw both locals and visitors alike, and they are also one of Aruba's only spots that will cook up your fresh fish catch for you. They are dog friendly,

Aruba signs like this one are found all over the island and are great spots for photo ops.

too. ✉ *Renaissance Marina, L. G. Smith Blvd. 82, Oranjestad* ☎ *297/746–4201* ⊕ *lucyssurf.com.*

★ The West Deck Island Grill Beach Bar

BARS | You'll find this casual wooden-decked beach bar along Linear Park facing Governor's Bay. Enjoy one of their special upside-down margaritas or incredible craft cocktails while you catch a stellar sunset and watch the cruise ships go by. After dark, the music takes it up a notch—sometimes live—and the atmosphere is fun and friendly. It's as popular with locals as it is with visitors. Great Caribbean tapas and grilled specialties are also on tap. ✉ *L. G. Smith Blvd at Governor's Bay Beach, Oranjestad ✛ Linear Park (next to the Queen Wilhelmina Park, adjacent to the Renaissance Suites)* ☎ *297/587–2667* ⊕ *www.thewestdeck.com.*

WEEKLY PARTIES
★ Bon Bini Festival

FESTIVALS | This year-round folklore event (the name means "welcome" in Papiamento) is held every Tuesday night (doors open at 6 pm, show starts at 7 pm) at Fort Zoutman in Oranjestad. In the inner courtyard, you can check out the Antillean dancers in resplendent costumes, feel the rhythms of the steel drums, browse among the stands displaying local artwork, and sample local food and drink. ✉ *Fort Zoutman, Zoutmanstraat z/n, Oranjestad* ☎ *297/588–5199* ⊕ *www.facebook.com/ArubaBonBiniFestival* 🎟 *$15.*

🛍 Shopping

Oranjestad's original "Main Street" (behind the Renaissance Wind Creek Resort Marina Hotel) has seen massive renovations of the entire Downtown region, which has breathed new life into the backstreets. A free ecotrolley transports cruise passengers to the Downtown core, but anyone can hop on and off to shop and stroll. Stores selling fashions, electronics, specialty items, sporting goods, and cosmetics can all be found on this renewed street, along with plenty of cafés, snack spots, and outdoor terraces where you can catch your breath between retail therapy jaunts. Low-duty luxury items can be found throughout Downtown's high-end shops, while authentic locally sourced and crafted souvenirs and knick-knacks are best sleuthed out at spots like the Local Market and the ArubaMade Mall.

DUTY-FREE STORES
Dufry

JEWELRY & WATCHES | No doubt you've seen this brand of duty-free stores in airports all over the world, but don't expect to see the same duty-free items like tobacco and spirits in this one. The prices are also not completely duty-free. What you will find are great bargains on cosmetics, perfumes, jewelry, and accessories from such brands as Carolina Herrera, Calvin Klein, Armani, Montblanc, and more. And there's always some kind of major sale on something of good quality going on here. There's another outlet in Royal Plaza Mall. ⊠ *G. F. Betico Croes 29, Oranjestad* ☎ *297/582–2790* ⊕ *www.dufry.com* ☉ *Closed Sun.*

ELECTRONICS
★ Boolchand's Digital World

ELECTRONICS | Family-run Boolchand's began in the 1930s and has since become a major retail institution throughout the Caribbean; they opened their first shop on Aruba in 1974. Today, their Downtown "Digital World" is your one-stop shop to get a high-tech fix at seriously low prices. Top-quality merchandise by major brands includes the latest in computers, cameras, and tech accessories, as well as quality watches and Pandora jewelry. ⊠ *Havenstraat 25, Oranjestad* ☎ *297/583–0147* ⊕ *boolchand.com* ☉ *Closed Sun.*

FOOD
Ling & Sons IGA Super Center

SUPERMARKET | Always a family-owned-and-operated grocery company, Ling and Sons adopted the IGA-brand supermarket-style with all the goods you would expect in an IGA back home. In addition to a wide variety of foods, there's a bakery, a deli, a butcher shop, and a well-stocked "liquortique." You can also order your groceries online to be delivered to your hotel room. The food court has excellent hot meals, including local fare. ■TIP→ **Ask about their VIP card for discounts and note that the store closes at 3 pm on Sunday.** ⊠ *Schotlandstraat 41, Oranjestad* ☎ *297/521–2370* ⊕ *www.lingandsons.com.*

GIFTS AND SOUVENIRS
★ Designs of Color by Dariana
ART GALLERIES | It's impossible not to be stopped in your tracks walking by this new art boutique in the Renaissance Marketplace due to the stunning original pieces showcased in the window. The thoughtfully curated and colorful collection of one-of-a-kind resin art sculptures and art pieces are not only ideal souvenirs, but also make wonderful top quality gifts. ⊠ *Renaissance Marketplace, L. G. Smith Blvd. 9, Oranjestad* ☎ *297/568–6283* ⊕ *www.themarket-placearuba.com* ☼ *Closed Sun.*

★ MOPA MOPA
CRAFTS | These shops specialize in original masks and crafty items called mopa mopa art. Originating with the Quillacinga people of Ecuador and Colombia, the art is made from the bud of the mopa mopa tree, boiled down into a resin, colored with dyes, and applied to carved mahogany and other woods like cedar. Masks, jewelry boxes, coasters, whimsical animal figurines, and more make wonderfully unique gifts and souvenirs. The masks are believed to ward off evil spirits. You can also buy works online. ⊠ *Renaissance Marketplace, L. G. Smith Blvd. 9, Oranjestad* ☎ *297/588–7297* ⊕ *www.mopamopaaruba.com* ☼ *Closed Sun.*

JEWELRY
Gandelman Jewelers
JEWELRY & WATCHES | Established in 1936, this family-run store is one of the island's premier jewelers. It's also Aruba's official Rolex retailer and the exclusive agent for names like Cartier (the only official retailer on the island), Patek Philippe, and David Yurman. ⊠ *Renaissance Mall, L. G. Smith Blvd. 82, Oranjestad* ☎ *297/529–9920* ⊕ *www.gandelman.net* ☼ *Closed Sun.*

★ Kay's Fine Jewelry
JEWELRY & WATCHES | Kay's family-run emporium is a well-known Aruba fixture on the fine-jewelry scene, and their designs have won awards. Exquisite settings featuring white and colored diamonds are their claim to fame, and they also have a fine selection of precious gems and brand-name timepieces. ⊠ *Weststraat 8, Oranjestad* ☎ *297/535–7467* ⊕ *www.kaysfinejewelry.com* ☼ *Closed Sun.*

Did You Know?

The Renaissance Marketplace has eclectic dining spots, trendy cafes, and live music nightly in their alfresco square.

Little Switzerland

With stores in the Royal Plaza Mall and one in Paseo Heren-cia—these well-known outlets specialize in designer jewelry and upscale timepieces by big-name designers like TAG Heuer, David Yurman, Breitling, Roberto Coin, Chopard, Pandora, Tiffany & Co., Cartier, Movado, Omega, and John Hardy. They also own the TAG Heuer Boutique in the Renaissance Mall. ⊠ *Royal Plaza Mall, L. G. Smith Blvd. 94, Oranjestad* ☏ *248/809–5560 ext. 40230* ⊕ *www. littleswitzerland.com.*

MALLS AND MARKETPLACES

The Local Market Aruba

MARKET | Focusing on locally made or inspired ware, this large out-door flea market across from the cruise terminal offers great deals on paintings, local music, cigars, sunglasses, local handicrafts, souvenirs and more, and the food trucks on-site are excellent. It closes at 6 pm. ⊠ *Between Paardenbaaistraat and Rockefeller-straat, in front of the cruise terminal, Oranjestad* ☏ *297/733–1982* ⊕ *www.facebook.com/thelocalmarketaruba/.*

★ Renaissance Mall

MALL | Upscale name-brand fashion and luxury brands of perfume, cosmetics, and leather goods are what you'll find in the array of 40 stores spanning two floors in this mall located within and underneath the Renaissance Wind Creek Resort Marina Hotel. You'll also find specialty items like cigars and designer shoes, plus high-end gold, silver, diamonds, and quality jewelry at low- or no-duty prices. Cafés and high-end dining, plus a casino and spa, round out the offerings. ⊠ *L. G. Smith Blvd. 12, Oranjestad* ☏ *297/523–6065* ⊕ *www.shoprenaissancearuba.com* ☉ *Closed Sun.*

★ Renaissance Marketplace

MALL | **FAMILY** | The Renaissance Marketplace is more of a dining and gathering spot along the marina than a market, though they do hold a weekly local artisans' outdoor market every Friday night. It's a lively spot with a few souvenir shops and specialty stores, and locals frequent the high-tech Arcade Aruba and the modern cinemas. But mostly it's full of eclectic dining emporiums and trendy cafés, and they have live music nightly in their alfresco square. The Renaissance Wind Creek Seaport Casino is also here, and it's steps from the cruise terminal on the marina. ⊠ *L. G. Smith Blvd. 9, Oranjestad* ☏ *297/583–6000* ⊕ *www.shoprenais-sancearuba.com.*

Royal Plaza Mall

MALL | It's impossible to miss this gorgeous colonial-style, cotton-candy-colored building with a big gold dome gracing the front street along the marina. It's one of the most photographed in Oranjestad. Three levels of shops (both indoors and out) make up this artsy arcade full of small boutiques, cigar shops, designer clothing outlets, gift and jewelry stores, and souvenir kiosks. Mojitos, a colorful second-story bar and restaurant, is popular with cruise visitors. ⊠ *L. G. Smith Blvd. 94, Oranjestad* ☎ *297/588–0351* ⊕ *www.aruba.com/us/explore/royal-plaza-mall* ⊙ *Closed Sun.*

PERFUMES AND COSMETICS

Penha, Dufry, Little Switzerland, and Maggy's are all known for their extensive fragrance offerings. Big brand names can often be found duty-free, too.

Penha

COSMETICS | Originating in Curaçao in 1865, Penha has branched out throughout the Caribbean and operates five stores on Aruba. The largest is right next to the Renaissance Wind Creek Resort Marina Hotel. The store is particularly known for good prices on high-end perfumes, cosmetics, skin-care products, eyewear, and fashions. You'll find brand names such as MAC, Lancôme, Estée Lauder, Clinique, Chanel, Dior, Montblanc, and Victoria's Secret, to name just a few. There is another Penha in Plaza Daniel Leo Downtown. ⊠ *Caya G. F. Betico Croes 11/13, Oranjestad* ☎ *297/582–0082* ⊕ *penhadutyfree.com* ⊙ *Closed Sun.*

MANCHEBO, DRUIF, AND EAGLE BEACHES

Updated by
Susan Campbell

⊙ Sights 🍽 Restaurants 🛏 Hotels 🛍 Shopping 🍸 Nightlife
★★★☆☆ ★★★★☆ ★★★★★ ★★☆☆☆ ★★☆☆☆

NEIGHBORHOOD SNAPSHOT

TOP EXPERIENCES

■ **Stroll Silky Sand:** Take long walks along a carpet of white sand capped with fiery sunsets.

■ **Dine Out in Style:** There's an eclectic array of unique dining locations: barefoot on the beach, canopied beds, or an intimate chef's table.

■ **Pamper Body and Soul:** Join beachfront yoga classes or partake in luxurious seaside massages.

■ **Dance Under the Stars:** Head to Alhambra Mall and Casino for live music at the alfresco restaurants and bars.

■ **Golf with Nature:** Play a picturesque round of golf amid ocean-view greens and beautifully landscaped lagoons.

GETTING HERE AND AROUND

The Eagle Beach region—also known as the low-rise section—is actually three beaches connected to each other, beginning right between the tip of Downtown Oranjestad just past the cruise-ship terminal and ending at the Bubali wetlands, just before the Divi Aruba Phoenix Beach Resort. It's about a 15-minute drive from the airport, and it's accessible by public bus from the Downtown terminal. There's free parking along the beaches.

PLANNING YOUR TIME

The best time to visit is during the day if you're seeking beach fun. There's no real nightlife, and except for the parties and entertainment for guests at the resorts, the Alhambra Mall and Casino is the only lively public place at night.

VIEWFINDER

■ Of course, the most iconic spot in this region is the emblematic Fofoti tree on Eagle Beach, but anywhere along that stretch will give you an ideal backdrop for your "I'm finally in paradise" pics. At **Divi's Beach Bar** on Druif Beach, you can watch the lively seabirds diving for fish at the "pelican poles." The picturesque poles are remnants of the old Eagle Refinery dock and the birds love to perch on them; it's also a good spot for "sunset over the sea" shots.

■ During the summer months, these beaches are the preferred nesting spot of big leatherback sea turtles, as they have been for 4,000 years. The island protects the nests with red and white wooden barriers, and if you're lucky you might see hatchlings scampering out of the sand and back to the sea.

Unlike the action-packed party that is Palm Beach, Eagle Beach is where you go to unwind, relax, recharge, and rejuvenate in pristine postcard-perfect settings. Once you experience it, you'll see why it's consistently rated among the top three beaches on the planet and you'll want to go back.

Nearby, an entire village of Divi resorts encompasses Druif Beach, while Manchebo Beach is the broadest stretch of sand on the island. It's become the spot for health and wellness retreats, and it's known to have the most eco-friendly hotel in the entire Caribbean. But the region is not without its opportunities to let loose and have some fun. The nexus for nighttime entertainment is the Alhambra Mall and Casino with lots of dining, bars, fast food, live music, and, of course, the casino. The Movies @ Gloria IMAX complex is in Eagle Beach and offers first-run movie diversions and its own dining, too.

◉ Sights

There are few attractions or historic sites in this region, but a new glassblowing factory and exhibit complex has added some extra culture to the area. Most pastimes are purely sun-and-sand oriented, romantic sunset dining and beach strolling; party activities typically center around the resorts.

The area's most famous sight is the Fofoti tree on Eagle Beach, the island's most photographed tree. It's the one that you so often see in Aruba's marketing and promotions; it's often mistakenly referred to as a divi-divi tree, and though similar, they are not the same species.

★ Lava Aruba Glass Studio
ARTS CENTER | The glassblowing company that opened this modern complex creates magnificent works using time-honored skills that trace back to Murano, Italy. They've been bringing the art of glassblowing to Venezuela through their family-run business since 1957, and now they are eager to educate Arubans and visitors alike by welcoming them into their open-space working factory to watch the masters create. There is also a spacious gallery where works

are available for purchase and a lovely café/bar on site. ✉ *Caya Harmonia 4, Sasakiweg, Eagle Beach* ☎ *287/280–3230* ⊕ *lavastudioaruba.com* 🎫 *Free* 🕑 *Closed Sun. Café closed Mon.*

★ The Movies @ Gloria

PERFORMANCE VENUE | Named after Teatro Gloria, Aruba's very first movie theatre built back in the 1930s, this entertainment complex now offers the most modern cinematic experience in the entire Caribbean. There are 10 cinemas in all, including IMAX and VIP theaters, and there's also a children's bouncy playground, a Starbucks, a huge food court, and stand-alone upscale dining options like P.F. Chang's, Olive Garden, and Sizzle Lounge. There are also special musical events with live bands and DJs. ✉ *Caya Dr. J. E. M. Arends 8, Eagle Beach* ☎ *297/523–6873* ⊕ *www.themoviesaruba.com/gloria-imax.*

CASINOS

★ Alhambra Casino

CASINO | Part of the Divi family and accessible by complimentary golf cart shuttle from all of the company's resorts except for Divi Phoenix, this is a lively popular casino with a big selection of modern slots, blackjack, craps, poker, roulette, and more. Be sure to join their Player's Club—it's free and offers free slot credits, and you earn points with your card as well. The Cove restaurant serves light meals and drinks; you'll also receive free drinks on the floor when you're playing the games. Special theme nights and promotions run all week. ✉ *J. E. Irausquin Blvd. 47, Druif* ☎ *297/588–9000* ⊕ *www.casinoalhambra.com.*

Beaches

Aruba's low-rise region is lined with beautiful beaches. Some have adopted the names of the resorts they are famous for: Manchebo Beach is technically the beginning of Eagle Beach, and Divi Beach is still Druif Beach, named for the type of trees that used to grow in abundance there. They join at Punta Brabo, which means "rough point"; it's aptly named, as the current and rip tides there can be severe and there's a quick drop-off. Eagle Beach continues in a long straight line afterward. It has often been named one of the world's top three beaches for good reason—it's postcard perfect. The surf is usually gentle but it can occasionally be rough, so heed the warning flags as there are no lifeguards.

Druif Beach

BEACH | **FAMILY** | Fine white sand and calm water make this beach a great choice for sunbathing and swimming. It's the base beach

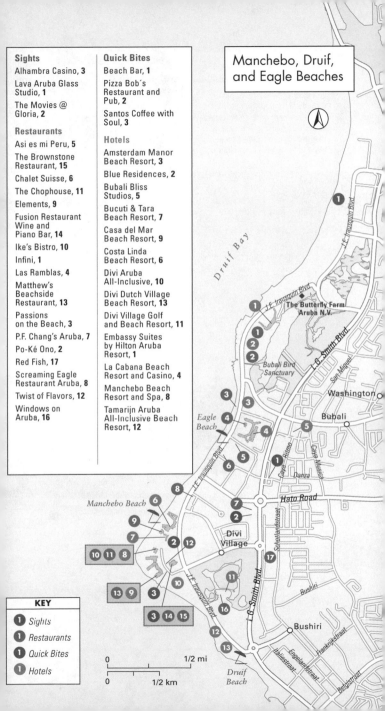

Sights

Alhambra Casino, **3**

Lava Aruba Glass Studio, **1**

The Movies @ Gloria, **2**

Restaurants

Asi es mi Peru, **5**

The Brownstone Restaurant, **15**

Chalet Suisse, **6**

The Chophouse, **11**

Elements, **9**

Fusion Restaurant Wine and Piano Bar, **14**

Ike's Bistro, **10**

Infini, **1**

Las Ramblas, **4**

Matthew's Beachside Restaurant, **13**

Passions on the Beach, **3**

P.F. Chang's Aruba, **7**

Po-Ké Ono, **2**

Red Fish, **17**

Screaming Eagle Restaurant Aruba, **8**

Twist of Flavors, **12**

Windows on Aruba, **16**

Quick Bites

Beach Bar, **1**

Pizza Bob´s Restaurant and Pub, **2**

Santos Coffee with Soul, **3**

Hotels

Amsterdam Manor Beach Resort, **3**

Blue Residences, **2**

Bubali Bliss Studios, **5**

Bucuti & Tara Beach Resort, **7**

Casa del Mar Beach Resort, **9**

Costa Linda Beach Resort, **6**

Divi Aruba All-Inclusive, **10**

Divi Dutch Village Beach Resort, **13**

Divi Village Golf and Beach Resort, **11**

Embassy Suites by Hilton Aruba Resort, **1**

La Cabana Beach Resort and Casino, **4**

Mancheboo Beach Resort and Spa, **8**

Tamarijn Aruba All-Inclusive Beach Resort, **12**

Manchebo, Druif, and Eagle Beaches

Druif Bay

The Butterfly Farm Aruba N.V.

J.E. Irausquin Blvd.

L.G. Smith Blvd.

Bubali Bird Sanctuary

San Miguel

Washington

Bubali

Eagle Beach

Caya Ruma

Caya Musica

Danza

Hato Road

Manchebo Beach

Divi Village

Scharlandstraat

Bushiri

Bushiri

J.E. Irausquin Blvd.

L.G. Smith Blvd.

Italiestraat

Frankrijkstraat

Druif Beach

Engelandstraat

Belgiestraat

0   1/2 mi

0   1/2 km

KEY

1 *Sights*

1 *Restaurants*

1 *Quick Bites*

1 *Hotels*

for the Divi collection of all-inclusive resorts, so amenities are reserved for guests, but the locals like it, too, and often camp out here with their own chairs and coolers. The beach is accessible by bus, rental car, or taxi, and it's within easy walking distance to many stores for food and drinks. The Beach Bar—owned by Divi Resorts but not part of the all-inclusive plan—is open to the public and is a superb spot to have lunch or early dinner, swim, and watch the sunset. **Amenities:** food and drink; toilets; parking (free); water sports. **Best for:** swimming; partiers. ⊠ *J. E. Irausquin Blvd., Druif* ✛ *Near the Divi resorts, south of Punta Brabo.*

★ Eagle Beach

BEACH | Aruba's most photographed stretch of sand, Eagle Beach is not only a favorite of visitors and locals, but also of sea turtles. More sea turtles nest here than anywhere else on the island. This pristine stretch of blinding white sand and aqua surf is ranked among the best beaches in the world. Many of the hotels have facilities on or near the beach, and refreshments are never far away; chairs and shade *palapas* are reserved for resort guests only. **Amenities:** food and drink; toilets; parking (no fee); water sports. **Best for:** sunsets; swimming. ⊠ *J. E. Irausquin Blvd., north of Manchebo Beach, Druif.*

★ Manchebo Beach (*Punta Brabo*)

BEACH | Impressively wide, the white-sand shoreline in front of the Manchebo Beach Resort (technically where Eagle Beach begins) is the backdrop for numerous yoga classes taking place under the giant palapa, as the resort offers health and wellness retreats. This sandy stretch is the broadest on the island; in fact you can even get a workout just getting to the water! Waves can be rough and wild at certain times of the year, so mind the current and undertow when swimming. **Amenities:** food and drink; toilets. **Best for:** swimming; sunset; walking. ■TIP→ **The Bucuti beach bar is reserved exclusively for guests of the Bucuti & Tara Beach Resort.** ⊠ *J. E. Irausquin Blvd., Druif* ✛ *At Manchebo Beach Resort.*

🍴 Restaurants

The Eagle Beach region has an eclectic selection of dining options, from high-end eateries to romantic private dining options and friendly beach bar haunts for burgers and barbecue. Many of the finest spots are part of resorts and are open to the public, but there are a few excellent stand-alone exceptions like Screaming Eagle, Windows on Aruba, and the chef's table experience at Infini.

Asi es mi Peru

$$$ | **PERUVIAN** | **FAMILY** | Owner Roxanna Salinas has created an authentic Peruvian-style dining spot to share a taste of her home with locals and visitors alike. Authentic specialties are artfully served in a warm and colorful enclave, and a portion of proceeds from the wares sold at the on-site Peruvian craft market go to a local Aruban cancer foundation. **Known for:** Peruvian-style ceviche made table-side; vegetarian and vegan menu available; chef's table experience upstairs. $ *Average main: $25* ✉ *Paradise Beach Villas, J. E. Irausquin Blvd. 64, Eagle Beach* ☎ *297/588–3958* ⊕ *asiesmiperuenaruba.com* ⊗ *Closed Mon.*

The Brownstone Restaurant

$$$ | **INTERNATIONAL** | Fashioned after a New York-style steak house and sports bar, the focus of The Brownstone is good stiff drinks, great steaks, and hearty portions of ribs, chicken, and fish. Pretentious it's not, but the fare is first-rate, and they have a well-curated selection of creative cocktails using only top-quality spirits. **Known for:** all-you-can eat ribs on Saturday; "Kibbeling" Night Monday (deep-fried beer battered grouper); friendly welcoming atmosphere and service. $ *Average main: $25* ✉ *Alhambra Mall, J. E. Irausquin Blvd. 47, Manchebo Beach* ☎ *297/280–7500* ⊕ *www.thebrownstonearuba.com* ⊗ *No lunch.*

Chalet Suisse

$$$$ | **EUROPEAN** | Opened in 1988 as a re-created Swiss-style chalet, this is a perennial favorite for its high-quality European dishes, excellent service, and warm inviting atmosphere. Old-school classics like chicken cordon bleu, beef Stroganoff, and duck à l'orange are still prepared to perfection here, and island-inspired favorites like Caribbean seafood platters keep it contemporary. **Known for:** expertly prepared whole rack of lamb; rich Swiss chocolate fondue for dessert; private Chalet Room for intimate dinners up to 16 people. $ *Average main: $40* ✉ *J. E. Irausquin Blvd. 246, Eagle Beach* ☎ *297/587–5054* ⊕ *www.chaletsuisse-aruba.com* ⊗ *Closed Sun. No lunch.*

★ The Chophouse

$$$$ | **INTERNATIONAL** | Low-key elegance and soft piano music set the stage for this indoor enclave where meaty chops and steaks are king and classic silver service is still in vogue. The big surprise here though is the chic Omakase Japanese Sushi Bar that shares the space, and their excellent creative selection of vegetarian, vegan, and gluten-free options. **Known for:** premium steaks and chops; predominately organic and sustainable fare; elegant old-world atmosphere combined with a modern sushi bar. $ *Average main: $45* ✉ *Manchebo Beach Resort, J. E. Irausquin Blvd. 55,*

Druif ☎ *297/522–3444* ⊕ *www.thechophousearuba.com* ⊗ *Sushi bar closed Sun.* ☞ *Credit cards only, no cash.*

★ Elements

$$$$ | CONTEMPORARY | A stellar spot with stunning seaside views, this strictly adults-only dining spot embodies the resort's global reputation for promoting green living and a healthy lifestyle. The wide-ranging menu of internationally flavored dishes includes many organic, vegan, vegetarian, and gluten-free choices that use locally sourced ingredients whenever possible. **Known for:** a la carte Sunday brunch; authentic Aruban and Caribbean buffet; romantic surfside atmosphere with private prix-fixe palapa dining. $ *Average main: $40* ⊠ *Bucuti and Tara Beach Resort, L. G. Smith Blvd. 55B, Eagle Beach* ☎ *297/583–1100* ⊕ *elementsaruba.com* ☞ *Credit cards only, no cash.*

★ Fusion Restaurant Wine and Piano Bar

$$$$ | INTERNATIONAL | What began as a classy laid-back wine and tapas piano bar has evolved into more of a New York–style steak lounge meets BBQ joint thanks to the popularity of the Big Green Egg BBQ trend. Once they began using this ceramic outdoor charcoal grill to offer up big, hearty, juicy cowboy steaks and grilled lobster tails, the aroma and smoke drew an entirely different kind of hungry and hearty crowd. **Known for:** Fusion special for two (22-oz. cowboy steak, 2 lobster tails, and wine); excellent selection of wine; creative "pair and share" tapas selections. $ *Average main: $45* ⊠ *Alhambra Mall, J. E. Irausquin Blvd, Druif* ☎ *297/280–9994* ⊕ *fusionaruba.com* ⊗ *Closed Sun. No lunch.*

★ Ike's Bistro

$$$ | INTERNATIONAL | A contemporary poolside dining option at Manchebo Beach Resort, this alfresco oasis features inspired Caribbean-international cuisine, and vegans are especially excited about their entire menu devoted to gourmet plant-based dining. Creative preparations of meat, seafood, and fish—locally sourced whenever possible—are all enhanced with flavors from the on-site herb garden, and the chef often surprises with exotic daily specials. **Known for:** paella night Thursday with Spanish music and live cooking; lobster and shrimp night Monday; Local Night Saturday with three- and four-course tasting menus. $ *Average main: $30* ⊠ *Manchebo Beach Resort, J. E. Irausquin Blvd. 55, Druif* ☎ *297/522–3444* ⊕ *www.ikesbistro.com* ☞ *Credit cards only, no cash.*

★ Infini

$$$$ | FUSION | Created in spring 2021 by legendary local chef Urvin Croes, one of the island's most innovative purveyors of ultra-modern cuisine, this new chef's table experience offers infinite possibilities for the palate. The "Chef's Impression" experience is an extensive 12-course themed menu based on world flavors and seasonal, locally sourced (whenever possible) ingredients; the plating of each dish is often so exquisite you might hesitate to dig in, but don't. **Known for:** chef and team personally talk you through the dining journey; wine and craft cocktail pairings for an extra charge; vegan or dietary restriction menus available with advance notice. $ *Average main: $149 ⊠ J.E. Irausquin Blvd. 266, Eagle Beach* ☎ *297/280–8869, 297/699–3982* ⊕ *infiniaruba.com* ☯ *Closed Mon. No lunch.*

Las Ramblas

$$$$ | SPANISH | This small alfresco Spanish-theme restaurant at La Cabana is often off-radar for anyone that's not a guest at the resort, but it's worth seeking out for excellent charcoal-grilled steaks and superb seafood paella. Even though it's not right on the water, you still can view stunning sunsets from its porch across the road from Eagle Beach. **Known for:** good selection of Spanish wines and homemade sangrias; excellent classic service; soft live guitar music or jazz and tiki torches make the setting very romantic. $ *Average main: $32 ⊠ La Cabana Beach Resort, J. E. Irausquin Blvd. 250, Eagle Beach* ☎ *297/520–1154* ⊕ *lacabana. com/en/pages/37* ☯ *Closed Sun. No lunch.*

Matthew's Beachside Restaurant

$$$ | INTERNATIONAL | The lively seaside eatery is popular with nonguests who make a special trip to enjoy great food (meats, fish, seafood, and a good selection of Italian specialties), superb sunsets, and the warm camaraderie of fun folks. It's a great place to catch the game or enjoy happy hour specials and snacks, and they serve breakfast and lunch, too. **Known for:** local fare on Wednesday; all-you-can-eat rib night on Tuesday; prix-fixe early-bird menu (except Tuesday). $ *Average main: $30 ⊠ Casa del Mar Beach Resort, J. E. Irausquin Blvd. 51, Manchebo Beach* ☎ *297/588–7300* ⊕ *www.matthews-aruba.com.*

★ Passions on the Beach

$$$$ | INTERNATIONAL | With stunning seafront sunsets and tiki torch lighting to enhance the mood, the signature restaurant of Amsterdam Manor is a favorite romantic escape for those seeking toes-in-the-sand dining. Popular with families (children under three eat free) and small groups as well, beachfront breakfasts and lunches are served on the deck. **Known for:** signature seafood platters; cashless payment; romantic toes-in-the-sand dining. $ *Average main: $45 ⊠ Amsterdam Manor Beach Resort, J. E. Irausquin Blvd. 252, Eagle Beach* ☎ *800/527–1118* ⊕ *amsterdammanor.com.*

P.F. Chang's Aruba

$$ | ASIAN | This massive, indoor-outdoor, well-known eatery promises "elevated Asian cuisine" as part of the Gloria entertainment venue, and it delivers. Especially popular for special occasions and family-style dinners, it's also a good spot for pre- or post-cinema meals. **Known for:** all dishes made from scratch with fresh ingredients; specialties from China, Japan, Korea, Thailand, and beyond; an eclectic selection of dim sum, handmade sushi, wok-fired bowls, and Asian-style noodles. ⑤ *Average main: $20 ⊠ Caya Dr. J. E. M. Arends 1, Eagle Beach* ☎ *297/523–6832* ⊕ *pfchangsaruba.aw.*

Po-Ké Ono

$$ | ASIAN | Tucked away in the lobby of Azure Residences on Eagle Beach, this is another culinary venture by legendary Chef Urvin Croes (owner of Infini), but here Croes strays from high-end upscale modern cuisine to create Asian comfort food. His fresh takes on poke, sushi, and steamed baos are inspired by his Chinese heritage; he also offers up some delicious vegan versions as well. **Known for:** authentic tuna poke; hoisin pork belly baos; Korean fried chicken. ⑤ *Average main: $15 ⊠ Azure Residences, J. E. Irausquin Blvd. 260, Eagle Beach* ☎ *297/525–3610* ⊕ *pokeonoaruba.com.*

Red Fish

$$ | CARIBBEAN | The owners of the legendary Downtown restaurant Driftwood and its sister operation, Driftwood Fishing Charters, opened this much smaller and far less formal dining nook centered around fresh fish and seafood. Locals love it and visitors are just beginning to discover it. **Known for:** authentic local experience; fresh fish and seafood by the pound; seafood pastas and paella. ⑤ *Average main: $15 ⊠ Orange Plaza Mall, Italiestraat 50, Druif* ⊹ *On the road directly behind the Divi golf course* ☎ *297/280–6666* ⊕ *www.redfisharuba.com* ☾ *Closed Mon.*

★ Screaming Eagle Restaurant Aruba

$$$$ | INTERNATIONAL | Not content to perch on its laurels as one of the most consistently highest-rated dining spots on the island, Screaming Eagle decided to reinvent itself to offer a more enticing alfresco experience by creating a toes-in-the sand dining experience without actually being at the beach! Thankfully, they haven't messed with the food, still serving up killer international fare indoors and out with an extensive wine list to match. **Known for:** excellent and eclectic selection of fresh fish and seafood dishes, as well as top-quality meats; crêpes Suzette prepared tableside; excellent wine cellar and multiple Wine Spectator awards. ⑤ *Average main: $45 ⊠ J. E. Irausquin Blvd. 228, Eagle Beach* ☎ *297/566–3050* ⊕ *screamingeaglearuba.com.*

★ Twist of Flavors

$$$ | **INTERNATIONAL** | **FAMILY** | There's always something cool happening at this bright and lively indoor-outdoor spot. The international kaleidoscopic menu includes everything from Dutch pancakes and Asian specialties to gourmet burgers and Caribbean seafood—surprisingly, they do it all very well. **Known for:** Thursday Grouper Nights; Friday (build-your-own) Burger Nights; Saturday prix fixe food and wine pairing specials. $ *Average main: $30* ✉ *Alhambra Mall, J. E. Irausquin Blvd. 47, Eagle Beach* ☎ *297/280– 2518* ⊕ *www.twistofflavorsaruba.com.*

★ Windows on Aruba

$$$$ | **INTERNATIONAL** | Overlooking Divi Village, this elegant indoor affair offers high-end international fare as well as their famous all-you-can-eat a la carte Royal Sunday Brunch that includes endless mimosas, gourmet surprises, dozens of enticing appetizers and sides, and lots of decadent desserts. They also serve a unique late-night brunch every Friday night with entertainment and cocktail specials. **Known for:** upscale gourmet fare; cosmopolitan bar area and stellar service; beautiful panoramic views from floor-to-ceiling windows. $ *Average main: $60* ✉ *Divi Village Golf and Beach Resort, J. E. Irausquin Blvd. 93, Druif* ☎ *297/523–5017* ⊕ *windowsonaruba.com* ☾ *Closed Mon.*

☕ Coffee and Quick Bites

★ Beach Bar

$$ | **INTERNATIONAL** | Located across the street from Divi Village Golf and Beach Resort, this trendy beachfront spot serves the perfect seaside casual fare—panini, wraps, burgers, and salads—as well as great cocktails and live entertainment. Enjoy superb swimming and sunset views there. **Known for:** excellent burgers, including vegan options; great tapas and colorful creative cocktails; double happy hours. $ *Average main: $15* ✉ *Druif Beach, J. E. Irausquin Blvd. 41, Druif* ☎ *297/583–5000* ⊕ *www.facebook. com/BeachBarAruba.*

Pizza Bob's Restaurant and Pub

$$ | **INTERNATIONAL** | **FAMILY** | Grab a slice, a whole pizza to go, or a cold beer and snack at this friendly alfresco hideaway beside the Alhambra Mall. There are also pasta dishes, salads, wraps, and BBQ options on the menu, as well as daily specials, and they deliver. **Known for:** great fried calamari; create-your-own pizza specials; Aruban-style pumpkin soup. $ *Average main: $15* ✉ *J. E. Irausquin Blvd. 57, Eagle Beach* ☎ *297/588–9040* ⊕ *www. facebook.com/pizzabobsaua/.*

Santos Coffee with Soul

$$ | INTERNATIONAL | Behind the Alhambra Mall, this is an ideal spot to get your gourmet coffee fix and grab some breakfast sandwiches to-go before a beach day. Or stop and chat with locals enjoying barista-style coffees, gourmet sandwiches, and decadent desserts at lunch. **Known for:** healthy smoothies and power breakfasts; special drinks of the month, like dulce de leche latte; friendly gathering spot. ⑤ *Average main: $12* ✉ *Casa del Mar (in front of parking lot), J. E. Irausquin Blvd. 51, Eagle Beach* ☎ *297/280–0303* ⊕ *santos-aruba.com.*

Hotels

Most hotels and resorts in this region were built to sprawl rather than tower, which is one reason why they call it the low-rise region. Most properties are no more than four stories tall, with a few exceptions like Blue Residences and the brand-new Embassy Suites by Hilton. The Divi resort family dominates the Druif Beach area with a collection of all-inclusives around their golf course.

Amsterdam Manor Beach Resort

$$ | HOTEL | FAMILY | Now with the distinction of being Aruba's only pet-friendly AAA Three Diamond hotel, Amsterdam Manor was first built in 1989 as a no-frills escape to attract Dutch visitors, especially families, seeking great value just steps from famed Eagle Beach. **Pros:** home to famous romantic restaurant Passions on the Beach; warm family-run atmosphere with superb staff and service; bright, clean, and eco-friendly oasis. **Cons:** not right on the beach; small pool; WaveRunners at beach can be noisy. ⑤ *Rooms from: $300* ✉ *Eagle Beach, J. E. Irausquin Blvd. 252, Eagle Beach* ☎ *297/527–1100, 800/969–2310* ⊕ *www.amsterdammanor.com* 🛏 *72 rooms* ⑩ *No Meals* ☞ *Cashless resort.*

Blue Residences

$$ | HOTEL | Bookended by Aruba's two most famous beaches (Eagle and Palm) on its own private man-made sandy strand right across the street, the Blue Residence Towers—one of three columns of condo hotel-style suites ranging from one to five bedrooms—offer epic unfettered views of the sea. **Pros:** full concierge services; all rooms have great sea views; lovely infinity pool looks out on the sea. **Cons:** not directly on the beach; far walk to shopping; little on-site entertainment. ⑤ *Rooms from: $350* ✉ *J. E. Irausquin Blvd. 266, Eagle Beach* ☎ *297/528–7000* ⊕ *bluearuba.com/resortblue-residences-properties* 🛏 *120 rooms* ⑩ *No Meals* ☞ *3-night minimum.*

Amsterdam Manor Beach Resort, a small hotel on Eagle Beach, is still family-run.

Bubali Bliss Studios

$ | HOTEL | Secreted behind Super Food Plaza, this economical and chic option is within walking distance of famed Eagle Beach, with beautifully decorated rooms (all of which have modern kitchens) and an inviting oasis pool surrounded by studios, deluxe studios, and one-bedroom apartments that are ideal for extended stays and work-cations. **Pros:** flexible anytime self-check-in and checkout; tropical pool garden with waterfall and hammocks; fully equipped kitchens. **Cons:** not on a beach; three-night minimum stay requirement; no on-site dining. $ *Rooms from: $205* ✉ *Bubali 147, Eagle Beach* ✛ *Behind Super Food Plaza* ☎ *297/587–5262* ⊕ *www.bubalibliss.com* ⇥ *10 rooms* ❖| *No Meals.*

★ Bucuti & Tara Beach Resort

$$$$ | HOTEL | Having achieved the first carbon-neutral status in the Caribbean, and winning multiple prestigious global eco awards, this landmark adults-only luxury boutique hotel offers exquisite personal service in an extraordinary beach setting. **Pros:** eco-friendly barefoot luxury at its best; unique arrival experience with personal concierge and iPad check-in; accessible management, with owners often on property. **Cons:** a little too quiet for some (no nighttime entertainment); pool is smaller than most hotels; not all rooms have sea views. $ *Rooms from: $585* ✉ *L. G. Smith Blvd. 55B, Druif* ☎ *297/583–1100* ⊕ *www.bucuti.com* ⇥ *104 rooms* ❖| *Free Breakfast.*

Fine white sand and calm water make Druif Beach a great place to sunbathe or swim.

Casa del Mar Beach Resort

$ | RESORT | FAMILY | The one- and two-bedroom suites at this beachside time-share resort are quite comfortable though not overly luxe. **Pros:** home-away-from-home feeling; family-friendly; popular Matthew's Beachside Restaurant is on-site. **Cons:** rooms feel a bit dated; charge for Wi-Fi; currents right offshore can be too strong for children. $ *Rooms from: $225* ✉ *J.E. Irausquin Blvd. 51, Manchebo Beach* ☎ *297/582–7000* ⊕ *casadelmar-aruba. com* 🔌 *147 rooms* ⍾ *No Meals.*

Costa Linda Beach Resort

$$$$ | RESORT | FAMILY | Operating like a small village unto itself, this all-suites, four-story, horseshoe-shaped time-share resort provides an ideal environment for families, with a kids' pool and colorful beachfront playground. **Pros:** spacious fully equipped suites; many activities available on-site; great beach. **Cons:** not all rooms have sea views; charge for Wi-Fi; some rooms are outdated. $ *Rooms from: $530* ✉ *J. E. Irausquin Blvd. 59, Eagle Beach* ☎ *297/583–8000* ⊕ *costalinda-aruba.com* 🔌 *155 rooms* ⍾ *No Meals.*

★ Divi Aruba All-Inclusive

$$$$ | RESORT | While the Tamarijn—Divi's sister property—caters mostly to families, this resort is favored more by couples and honeymooners. **Pros:** on a wonderful stretch of beach; eclectic choice of dining and entertainment; cosmopolitan lively vibe. **Cons:** some older rooms are small by modern standards; not all rooms have sea views; reservations mandatory for the more upscale restaurants. $ *Rooms from: $832* ✉ *J. E. Irausquin Blvd. 45, Druif*

☎ 297/525–5200, 800/554–2008 ⊕ www.diviandtamarijnaruba. com ⮌ 261 rooms ⦿ All-Inclusive ☞ 3- or 5-night minimum.

Divi Dutch Village Beach Resort

$$$ | HOTEL | FAMILY | This modern all-suite resort features very spacious, fully equipped accommodations ideal for families and small groups wishing to self-cater; there's also an all-inclusive option that gives access to all the food and drink at both Divi Aruba and the Tamarijn, and they now also offer a breakfast plan. **Pros:** family-friendly wading pools; spacious suites fully equipped with modern appliances; supermarkets are within walking distance. **Cons:** not directly on the beach; no ocean views from most rooms; no nightly entertainment unless you go to sister resorts. ⑤ *Rooms from: $465* ✉ *J. E. Irausquin Blvd. 47, Druif* ☎ *297/583–5000, 800/367–3484* ⊕ *www.diviresorts.com* ⮌ *123 rooms* ⦿ *No Meals* ☞ *All-inclusive options has a 3-night minimum.*

Divi Village Golf and Beach Resort

$$$ | RESORT | FAMILY | All the rooms at this all-suites golf resort community across the street from Druif Beach include fully equipped kitchens, but an all-inclusive option is also available with access and shuttles to sister resorts Tamarijn, Divi Aruba, and Divi Dutch Village. **Pros:** excellent golf course; dedicated beach space with lounge chairs and shade palapas across the street; lush and lovely grounds with freshwater lagoons and wildlife. **Cons:** no suites have two beds, only one bed and a sleeper sofa; the resort is not beachfront; no ocean-view rooms. ⑤ *Rooms from: $455* ✉ *J. E. Irausquin Blvd. 93, Druif* ☎ *297/583–5000* ⊕ *www. diviresorts.com* ⮌ *348 rooms* ⦿ *All-Inclusive* ☞ *3-night minimum for all-inclusive.*

Embassy Suites by Hilton Aruba Resort

$$ | RESORT | The first new resort built on the island in ages, this sprawling high-rise property opened its doors in 2023 with modern, smartly designed efficiency suites decorated in Caribbean color accents and food and beverage options provided by the brand's signature Brickstone outlets. **Pros:** all-suite resort; free made-to-order breakfasts and daily complimentary cocktail evening receptions; massive pool and spacious lounging areas. **Cons:** access to the beach is via a tunnel under the road; little entertainment; no umbrellas provided with beach chairs. ⑤ *Rooms from: $285* ✉ *J. E. Irausquin Blvd. 268, Eagle Beach* ☎ *297/525–6000* ⊕ *www.hilton.com* ⮌ *330 rooms* ⦿ *Free Breakfast.*

La Cabana Beach Resort and Casino

$ | **RESORT** | **FAMILY** | This warm and friendly complex of mostly time-share units draws repeat visitors (primarily families) who enjoy the spacious and recently renovated accommodations equipped with everything needed for a home away from home, including a fully equipped kitchen. **Pros:** lively family-friendly atmosphere with large pool facilities; the only on-resort chapel on the island; laundry facilities on every floor. **Cons:** you have to cross the road to get to the beach; limited number of shade palapas; few rooms have sea views. ⑤ *Rooms from: $209* ✉ *J. E. Irausquin Blvd. 250, Eagle Beach* ☎ *297/520–1100* ⊕ *lacabana.com* ⇨ *449 rooms* ⦿l *No Meals.*

Manchebo Beach Resort and Spa

$$$ | **RESORT** | One of the original low-rise resorts built on Aruba has refreshed and reinvented itself over the past few years to become a dedicated health and wellness boutique resort with daily complimentary seafront yoga, Pilates classes, and healthy and healing cuisine menus. **Pros:** located on the island's broadest and most pristine white-sand beach; all-inclusive meal plans available; great on-site restaurants and culinary events. **Cons:** rooms are on the small side; not much in way of entertainment; not all rooms have sea views. ⑤ *Rooms from: $425* ✉ *J. E. Irausquin Blvd. 55, Manchebo Beach* ☎ *297/522–3444* ⊕ *www.manchebo.com* ⇨ *72 rooms* ⦿l *No Meals.*

★ Tamarijn Aruba All-Inclusive Beach Resort

$$$$ | **RESORT** | **FAMILY** | Having received a major multimillion-dollar refresh in 2021, the interiors of this popular all-inclusive almost rival the stellar sea scenes that are mere steps from each oceanfront room. **Pros:** complimentary shuttle service between Divi resorts and the Alhambra Casino and Mall; children 12 and under stay and eat free; complimentary Sea Turtles Club for kids. **Cons:** beach entrance can be rocky (beach shoes recommended); no room service; main pool can become crowded. ⑤ *Rooms from: $832* ✉ *J. E. Irausquin Blvd. 41, Punta Brabo* ☎ *297/525–5200, 800/554–2008* ⊕ *www.diviandtamarijnaruba.com/tamarijn-rooms.htm* ⇨ *261 rooms* ⦿l *All-Inclusive* ⌾ *3-night minimum.*

Nightlife

Most of the nightlife in this area revolves around the resorts, where there are often special shows and live music for guests around pool areas. Some of their beach bars have regular special events like karaoke nights (the public is usually welcome). But there are a few standout stand-alone night spots if you know where to go.

BARS
Coco Loco Beach Bar and Restaurant
BARS | Just past Costa Linda Beach Resort, traveling toward the high-rise area, keep your eyes peeled for this colorful stand-alone beach shack that pops up out of nowhere on Eagle Beach. If you see a life-sized Captain Morgan outside, you'll know you're in the right spot! It's the quintessential colorful Caribbean-style beach bar by day, offering up snacks and tropical drinks, even shaved ice and fresh coconut water. As the sun begins to set it comes to life as a hot party spot, luring folks to come dance barefoot in the sand to DJ-driven or live music. Beach lounges and umbrellas are available during the day if you want to take advantage of that prime Eagle Beach real estate while you indulge. ✉ *J. E. Irausquin Blvd 67A, Eagle Beach* ☎ *297/280–8081* ⊕ *www.facebook.com/ cocolocobeachbar.*

★ Horizons Lounge
COCKTAIL LOUNGES | It's worth it to sleuth out this delightful little alfresco cocktail lounge, located up the stairs from Amsterdam Manor's pool, to enjoy their excellent cocktail offerings and the unparalleled view of the famed Fofoti tree on Eagle Beach at sunset. There's soft live music and a second happy hour at 9 pm, as well as a diverse selection of bites or hearty meals if you're inclined to stay for dinner (think macadamia grouper, lamb cutlets, or vegan beef gnocchi). ✉ *Amsterdam Manor Beach Resort, J. E. Irausquin 252, Eagle Beach* ☎ *287/527–1118* ⊕ *www.amsterdam-manor.com.*

Shopping

This region isn't known for great shopping, though all the resorts have their own little stores and the area has the island's largest supermarkets—good to know if you're self-catering. But do check out the weekly arts and crafts market on Tuesday nights at Santos Coffee with Soul; all vendors are local artisans and make excellent souvenirs.

CLOTHING AND ACCESSORIES
★ The Lazy Lizard
OTHER SPECIALTY STORE | Fun and trendy beachwear and resort fashions are sold here, along with accessories like fancy flip-flops, sandals, Aruba-inspired T-shirts, and totes for the whole family. There are souvenirs as well. ✉ *Alhambra Mall, Eagle Beach* ☎ *297/592–7805* ⊕ *www.thelazylizard.com.*

MALLS AND MARKETPLACES
★ The Shops at Alhambra Mall

SHOPPING CENTER | There's an eclectic array of shops and dining in alfresco Alhambra Mall with the casino as its focal point. Dotted with small retail stores, souvenir shops, and a mini-market, the mall also has multiple fast-food outlets as well as finer dining options like Fusion Wine and Piano Bar, The Brownstone Restaurant, and Twist of Flavors. There's live music at some spot every night, and there's also a small spa. Stores are open late, and the casino is open until the wee hours. ⊠ *J. E. Irausquin Blvd. 47, Druif* ☎ *297/583–5000* ⊕ *www.facebook.com/alhambrashops.*

★ Super Food Plaza

SHOPPING CENTER | This massive complex offers all kinds of extras; it's more like a small department store. Beyond a huge fresh produce section, fresh fish and seafood market, bakery, and deli section, there's also a café, a drugstore, and even a toy store on site. It's truly a one-stop shop for all your needs. There's even an excellent selection of vegan products. They also deliver, and you can shop online and order curbside pickup, too. **■TIP→ Even if you are only on island for a week, chances are good you will make more than one visit here, so first trip, stop by the customer service desk and ask for a Bonus Card to save on all kinds of products and take advantage of weekly specials.** ⊠ *Bubali 141-A, Eagle Beach* ☎ *297/522–2000* ⊕ *www.superfoodaruba.com.*

PALM BEACH AND NOORD AND WESTERN TIP (CALIFORNIA DUNES)

Updated by
Susan Campbell

◉ Sights   🍴 Restaurants   🛏 Hotels   🛍 Shopping   🍸 Nightlife

★★★★☆   ★★★★☆   ★★★★☆   ★★★★☆   ★★★★☆

NEIGHBORHOOD SNAPSHOT

TOP EXPERIENCES

■ **Swim, Stroll, People-Watch:** The island's liveliest stretch of sand and sea is unfettered by barriers or barricades.

■ **Water Sports Galore:** There's a wide assortment of water sports available along Palm Beach.

■ **Electric Tropical Nights:** "The Strip" is full of bars, restaurants, cafés, and shops.

■ **Go Casino-Hopping:** Most high-rise hotels have their own glitzy casino, so you can hop from one to another without a car.

■ **Visit the Western Tip:** Climb the historic California Lighthouse and explore the cool sand dunes surrounding it.

GETTING HERE AND AROUND

Palm Beach, part of the larger Noord region, is the island's liveliest tourism area and home to all the high-rise hotels.

Depending on traffic, it's about 25 minutes from the airport to the Palm Beach/Noord area; there's no public bus service directly from the airport. To avoid Downtown traffic, Watty Vos Boulevard (completed in 2019) provides a direct route from the airport to Palm Beach. If you're driving, be aware that there are a lot of roundabouts to navigate.

There's plenty of free parking around the high-rise hotels and beach area, as well as paid lots. Public buses from the Arubus terminal in Oranjestad stop at every major resort. Shared transport vans and private transfer options are available, as are taxis.

VIEWFINDER

■ This region has plenty of paradisiacal beach scenes to capture, including the California Lighthouse—try it at sunrise instead of sunset for a whole different vibe—and the panoramic views from Alto Vista Chapel. There are also a few "I Love Aruba" type signs lit up at night along the Palm Beach strip for fun souvenir pics, and The Butterfly Farm has a wing mural wall and colorful adult-sized butterfly wings you can don for the ideal souvenir photo.

NOORD

■ Once away from the hotels, Noord is all local neighborhoods with scenic little beach coves and sand dunes skirting the coast, culminating at the famous California Lighthouse. The little cove at Malmok is known for spotting sea turtles and starfish.

Soft white sand for miles, clear aqua surf, lively beach bars, exciting water sports, fine dining, world-class casinos, superb shopping, electric nightlife, first-rate resorts—it's all within a stone's throw in Palm Beach. So park your car and get ready to pleasure-hop your way through Aruba's liveliest beach region, no matter the time of day or night.

Palm Beach and Noord

The district of Noord is home to the bulk of the high-rise hotels and casinos that line Palm Beach. The hotels and restaurants, ranging from haute cuisine to fast food, are densely packed into a few miles running along the beachfront, while the bulk of the nightlife takes place along J. E. Irausquin Boulevard, also known as "The Strip." When other areas of Aruba are shutting down for the night, this area is guaranteed to still be buzzing with activity.

The Cove Mall is an entire block of trendy bars and dining spots that allow you to take your taste buds on an international tour. It's also an excellent place to begin an electric night on foot before you head on down The Strip.

Don't be afraid to venture outside of the tourism epicenter, though, because pristine wild coastal scenes and charming local neighborhoods await. You'll also find attractions like Philip's Animal Garden in the outskirts.

Sights

★ Aruba Etnia Nativa

OTHER MUSEUM | Take a deep dive into Aruba's history, culture, and heritage as you walk among the gardens and the interior of this home/museum/gallery. On the personal one-hour guided tour (cash only), get a behind-the-scenes look and hear folk stories about the island's journey from Amerindian to colonial past, through industrial endeavors all the way up to today's tourism landscape. This operation also produces "Island-Insight" for

Sights

Aruba Etnia Nativa, **1**

Bubali Bird Sanctuary, **10**

Butterfly Farm, **9**

The Casino Aruba, **8**

The Casino at The Ritz-Carlton, Aruba, **2**

The Cove Mall, **4**

Hyatt Regency Casino, **6**

Liv Casino, **7**

Philip's Animal Garden, **11**

Stellaris Casino, **3**

Xanadu, **5**

Restaurants

Agave Mexican Cuisine, **6**

Aqua Grill, **19**

Atardi, **3**

Azia Restaurant Lounge, **17**

Bavaria Food & Beer, **21**

BLT Steak, **2**

Bohemian, **16**

Brutto Aruba, **20**

Campeones Cantina and Tequila Bar, **5**

Casa Nonna, **1**

Da Vinci Ristorante, **7**

Fireson Brewing Company, **9**

Hanasaki Fusion, **26**

Hostaria Da' Vittorio, **22**

The Journey, **28**

King Fred & Princess Diana, **27**

The Lazy Turtle, **13**

Madame Janette, **31**

MooMba Beach Bar and Restaurant, **8**

Old Cunucu House, **23**

Papiamento, **25**

Papillon, **18**

pureocean, **29**

Quinta del Carmen, **30**

Rotisserie La Braise, **12**

Ruinas del Mar, **14**

Ruth's Chris Steak House, **4**

Senses Fine Dining, **10**

Sunset Grille, **15**

2 Fools and a Bull Gourmet Studio, **24**

The Vue Rooftop Restaurant and Bar, **11**

Quick Bites

Drunk's Denial, **3**

Eduardo's Beach Shack, **1**

Scott's Brats, **2**

Hotels

Aruba Marriott Resort and Stellaris Casino, **3**

Barceló Aruba, **9**

Boardwalk Boutique Hotel Aruba, **1**

Courtyard Aruba Resort by Marriott, **14**

Divi Aruba Phoenix Beach Resort, **12**

Hilton Aruba Caribbean Resort and Casino, **10**

Holiday Inn Resort Aruba, **5**

Hotel Riu Palace Antillas, **13**

Hotel Riu Palace Aruba, **11**

Hyatt Regency Aruba Resort, Spa, and Casino, **8**

Marriott's Aruba Ocean Club, **4**

Playa Linda Beach Resort, **6**

Radisson Blu Aruba, **7**

The Ritz-Carlton, Aruba, **2**

KEY	
1	*Sights*
1	*Restaurants*
1	*Quick Bites*
1	*Hotels*

0 — 1/2 mi

0 — 1/2 km

Druif Bay

Eagle Beach

J.E. Irausquin Blvd.

Manchebo Beach

Divi Village

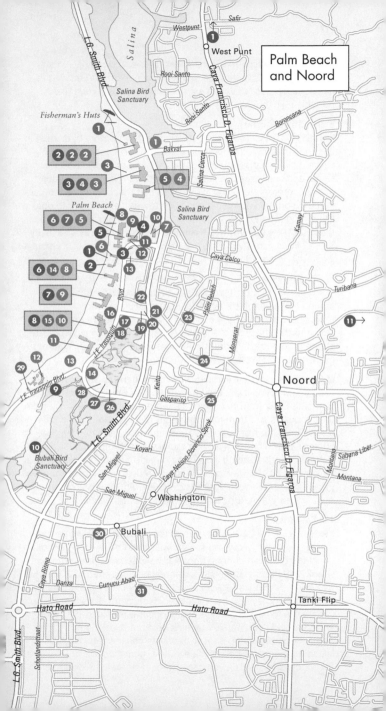

Palm Beach
and Noord

the English newspaper *Aruba Today*. ⊠ *Westpunt 37A, Noord* ☎ *297/592–2702 WhatsApp* ⊕ *www.facebook.com/EtniaNativa* ⊠ *$35 (cash only)* ⚄ *By appointment only* ☞ *Maximum 4-5 people*.

Bubali Bird Sanctuary

NATURE PRESERVE | More than 80 species of migratory birds nest in this man-made wetland area inland from the island's strip of high-rise hotels. Herons, egrets, cormorants, coots, gulls, skimmers, terns, and ducks are among the winged wonders in and around the two interconnected artificial lakes that make up the sanctuary. Perch up on the wooden observation tower for great photo ops. (Bring bug repellent as the area is marshy and attracts mosquitoes.) ∎**TIP**➔ **Go early in the morning to see the most avian activity.** ⊠ *J. E. Irausquin Blvd., Noord* ⊕ *www.aruba.com/us/explore/bubali-bird-sanctuary* ⊠ *Free*.

★ Butterfly Farm

FARM/RANCH | **FAMILY** | Hundreds of butterflies and moths from around the world flutter about this spectacular garden. Guided tours (included in the price of admission) provide an entertaining look into the life cycle of these insects, from egg to caterpillar to chrysalis to butterfly or moth. After your initial visit, you can return as often as you like for free during your vacation.

∎**TIP**➔ **Go early in the morning when the butterflies are most active; wear bright colors if you want them to land on you.** Early morning is also when you are most likely to see the caterpillars emerge from their cocoons and transform into butterflies or moths. The little Nectar Café out front serves refreshing drinks and homemade popsicles. Don't miss the wing mural wall and the adult-size butterfly wings hanging in the tree outside, free to wear and ideal for photos. ⊠ *J. E. Irausquin Blvd., Palm Beach* ⊹ *across from Divi Phoenix Aruba Beach Resort* ☎ *297/586–3656* ⊕ *www.facebook.com/butterflyfarmaruba* ⊠ *$16 (good for return visits)*.

The Cove Mall

STORE/MALL | The Cove Mall is an entire block of trendy bars and dining spots that allow you to take your taste buds on an international tour. You can choose from Asian, Mexican, French, Italian, Greek, and international comfort foods here; opened in 2023, the well-known American Italian brand Patrizia's chain chose this spot as their first foray into the Caribbean. New North End Pub and Grill caters to casual partiers and brings live music to the block, while second-floor The Vue takes it up a notch as the island's only rooftop bar/dining spot with private cabanas and hot DJs. Island-brewed craft beer and decadent munchies live at Fireson's Brewing Company, but you can also get your healthy on too at Yolo

Rainforest Cafe. The Cove Mall has truly become Palm Beach's anchor of action and an excellent place to begin an electric night on foot before you head on down The Strip. ⊠ *J. E. Irausquin Blvd. 384A, Palm Beach ✛ Across the street from Holiday Inn* ☎ *297/586–8191* ⊕ *www.facebook.com/thecovearuba.*

★ Philip's Animal Garden

FARM/RANCH | **FAMILY** | This nonprofit exotic animal rescue and reha-bilitation foundation is a wonderful child-friendly attraction you'll find just off the beaten track up in Noord. Each guest is given a bag of treats for the animal residents, which include monkeys, peacocks, an emu, an ocelot, an alpaca, and many other types of creatures you're not likely to see elsewhere on Aruba. There's a large playground and ranch so little ones can run. It is also a stop on some tours. ⊠ *Alto Vista 116, Noord* ☎ *297/593–5363* ⊕ *www. philipsanimalgarden.com* 🎫 *$10.*

CASINOS

The Casino Aruba

CASINO | This modern Vegas-style casino offers all the latest gaming options, upgraded machines, and lots of betting action like blackjack, poker, and roulette. Every day there is a different promotion or special for their VIP Players Club members (free of charge to join) and frequent poker tournaments. ⊠ *Hilton Aruba Caribbean Resort, J. E. Irausquin Blvd. 81, Palm Beach* ☎ *297/526–6930* ⊕ *www.tcaruba.com.*

★ The Casino at The Ritz-Carlton, Aruba

CASINO | A very "ritzy" casino just off the lobby of The Ritz-Carlton, Aruba offers many traditional table games like blackjack, craps, roulette, Caribbean stud poker, baccarat, and Texas Hold'em and close to 300 snazzy modern slots: spinning reels, video reels, and video games with jackpots. This 24-hour spot also has two sports-betting kiosks and offers "luxury" bingo several times a week. Points accumulated from their VIP casino club card can also be used toward hotel extras like dining, spa treatments, and room nights. ⊠ *L. G. Smith Blvd. 107, Palm Beach* ☎ *297/527–2222* ⊕ *www.ritzcarlton.com/en/hotels/auart-the-ritz-carlton-aruba/ experiences/.*

Hyatt Regency Casino

CASINO | One of the island's smaller gaming spots but just as glitzy, this lively casino offers 13 gaming tables, 148 slot machines, and 13 video poker machines. Be sure to join their Play-er's Advantage Club for all kinds of free play and point promotions. ⊠ *Hyatt Regency Aruba Resort, Spa, and Casino, J. E. Irausquin Blvd. 85, Palm Beach* ☎ *297/586–1234* ⊕ *aruba.regency.hyatt.com.*

Liv Casino

CASINO | A small but welcoming little casino is just off the lobby of Barceló Aruba Resort. It's a great spot to try your luck at some of the most modern slot games. They also have blackjack and roulette, and there are also some interesting promotions every week. ⊠ *Barceló Aruba Resort, J. E. Irausquin Blvd. 83, Palm Beach* ☎ *297/280–4000* ⊕ *www.facebook.com/LivCasinoAruba.*

★ Stellaris Casino

CASINO | One of the island's largest casinos is open 24 hours a day and offers 500 modern interactive slots, as well as 26 tables with games like craps, roulette, poker, and blackjack. There's also a state-of-the-art race and sports betting operation. Don't forget to join the VIP Club program, where you can earn points, comps, and prizes. They offer free cocktails for gamers, and there are many special theme and entertainment nights. ⊠ *Aruba Marriott Resort, L. G. Smith Blvd. 101, Palm Beach* ☎ *297/586–9000* ⊕ *www.stellariscasino.com.*

Xanadu

CASINO | Opened in late 2022, this modern space in the Holiday Inn is bright and cheery with a welcoming staff. The casino boasts 186 new slot machines, Moneyball sports betting, table games, and a poker room. A Players Club and free parking add to the allure. ⊠ *Holiday Inn Resort Aruba, J. E. Irausquin Blvd 230, Noord* ☎ *297/288–4400* ⊕ *www.xanadu-casino.com.*

Beaches

Fisherman's Huts (*Hadicurari*)

BEACH | Beside the Ritz-Carlton, Fisherman's Huts (aka Hadicurari Beach) is a windsurfer, kiteboarder, and now "wing-foiling" haven. Swimmers might have a hard time avoiding all the boards going by; as this is the nexus of where the lessons take place for these water sports, it's always awash in students, experts, and board hobbyists. It's a gorgeous spot to just sit and watch the sails on the sea, and lately it's become increasingly popular among paddleboarders and sea kayakers, too. Only drinks and small snacks are available at the operator's shacks. There are no restrooms, but the Ritz lobby is nearby in a pinch. **Amenities:** food and drink; parking (free); water sports. **Best for:** windsurfing. ⊠ *L. G. Smith Blvd., Palm Beach.*

★ Palm Beach

BEACH | This is the island's most populated and popular beach running along the high-rise resorts, and it's crammed with every kind of water-sport activity and food-and-drink emporium imaginable.

It's always crowded no matter the season, but it's a great place for people-watching, sunbathing, swimming, and partying; there are always activities happening, like paddleboarding and even paddleboard yoga and Pilates. The water is pond-calm; the sand, powder-fine. **Amenities:** food and drink; showers; toilets; water sports. **Best for:** partiers; swimming. ⊠ *J. E. Irausquin Blvd., Palm Beach* ✛ *between Divi Aruba Phoenix Beach Resort and Ritz-Carlton, Aruba.*

🍴 Restaurants

★ Agave Mexican Cuisine

$$ | **MEXICAN** | Named after the plant tequila is derived from, this welcome addition to Aruba's culinary scene is dedicated to showcasing authentic Mesoamerican flavors inspired by diverse regions like Oaxaca. Familiar-sounding dishes like tacos, tostadas, enchiladas, and fajitas come full of surprises like braised octopus, beef tongue, chorizo, and cotija cheese, and they also do a mean vegan taco. **Known for:** creative Mesoamerican-inspired specialties; delicious desserts like salted caramel churros and tres leches cake with a twist; mixologists creating personal signature concoctions for guests. ⑤ *Average main: $20* ⊠ *Holiday Inn Aruba Resort, J. E. Irausquin Blvd 230, Noord* ☎ *297/586–3600* ⊕ *www. holidayarubaresort.com/en/agave-mexican-cuisine/* ⊙ *Closed Mon., Wed., Fri., and Sun. No lunch.*

Aqua Grill

$$$$ | **SEAFOOD** | Aficionados flock here to enjoy a wide selection of seafood and fish in a New England–style decor. Dishes like smoked swordfish, Maine lobster, and grilled red snapper are top of the list, or try a bit of everything with the Fisherman's Pot. **Known for:** daily fresh seafood, either from local fishermen or flown in; massive raw bar; oysters on the half shell. ⑤ *Average main: $40* ⊠ *J. E. Irausquin Blvd. 374, Palm Beach* ☎ *297/586–5900* ⊕ *aqua-grill.com* ⊙ *No lunch.*

Atardi

$$$$ | **INTERNATIONAL** | This rollicking beach bar by day morphs into a surprisingly romantic pop-up, toes-in-the-sand dining spot as soon as the sun begins to set—the sunsets rarely disappoint. Fresh fish and seafood are the specialty but meat lovers will be well sated with the excellent filet mignon and short ribs dishes. **Known for:** sunset and torchlit seaside dining; attentive personal service; excellent fish and seafood. ⑤ *Average main: $55* ⊠ *Aruba Marriott Resort and Stellaris Casino, L. G. Smith Blvd. 101, Palm Beach* ☎ *297/520–6537* ⊕ *www.atardiaruba.com.*

Did You Know?

Aruba's beaches are legendary: the solid seven miles of beachfront along its west coast are baby-powder soft, blindingly white sand carpets that smile over vast expanses of clear azure water.

★ Azia Restaurant Lounge

$$$$ | ASIAN FUSION | Secreted away just off the main Palm Beach strip, seek out the hidden Buddha to find the twinkling lights that lead to an absolutely enchanting upscale Asian-fusion emporium with stunning decor and Aruba's longest bar. Enjoy an eclectic selection of dim sum, sushi, and creative meat and seafood dishes that can be paired with sake, Japanese beer, and whiskey or a killer handcrafted cocktail from their expert mixologists. **Known for:** great for groups as it seats 350 and has excellent shareables; semiprivate room for up to 12 people is unique to the island; excellent sushi. ⑤ *Average main: $32* ⊠ *J. E. Irausquin Blvd. 348, Palm Beach* ✢ *Across the street from the Hilton* ☎ *297/586–0088* ⊕ *www.aziaaruba.com.*

Bavaria Food & Beer

$$$ | GERMAN | A variety of German beers, schnitzel, and bratwurst presented in a true beer-hall setting are guaranteed to provide that Oktoberfest feeling. The hearty cuisine is paired with over 20 different types of beer by owners who take their imbibing seriously. **Known for:** German cuisine served in an "oom-pa-pa" atmosphere; fun and friendly crowd of locals and visitors; outdoor beer garden suitable for large groups. ⑤ *Average main: $25* ⊠ *Palm Beach 186B, Noord* ☎ *297/586–8550* ⊕ *www.bavaria-aruba.com* ☉ *Closed Sun.*

BLT Steak

$$$$ | AMERICAN | Though this restaurant in the Ritz-Carlton is designed to replicate a New York–style steak house, if you're looking for a more Caribbean feel, opt for the ethereal dining room that leads out to a breezy garden terrace just steps from the sea for stellar sunset views that are unmistakably Caribbean. And though it's supposed to be all about the meat here, their very pricey but comprehensive seafood platter called The Royale is worth the splurge. **Known for:** 28-day dry-aged porterhouse for two; USDA Prime 100% naturally raised certified Black Angus beef; surprising selection of East and West Coast oysters. ⑤ *Average main: $60* ⊠ *The Ritz-Carlton, Aruba, L. G. Smith Blvd. 107, Palm Beach* ☎ *297/527–2399* ⊕ *www.bltrestaurants.com/location/blt-steak-aruba/* ☉ *No lunch.*

★ Bohemian

$$$$ | INTERNATIONAL | Secreted away near the Barceló resort you'll find a hip, laid-back tropical oasis of tiki-style huts and "bohemian" escapes with a focus on French and world cuisine, sometimes with a local Caribbean twist. It's well worth seeking out for the cool vibe and eclectic choice of fare, ranging from raclette or ginger-and-honey duck to braised lamb or paella, with some creative

vegetarian and vegan options thrown in. **Known for:** fresh mussels flown in from Holland when available; house-made foie gras and excellent charcuterie and cheese plates; first-rate trendy bar and craft cocktails. $ *Average main: $45* ⊠ *J. E. Irausquin Blvd. 83, Palm Beach* ✛ *Beside the Barceló* ☎ *297/280-8448* ⊕ *bohemianaruba.com* ⊙ *No lunch.*

★ Brutto Aruba

$$$$ | **INTERNATIONAL** | Seeking to capture the quintessential hip experience, Brutto is trendy on steroids—think cocktails served in biodegradable plastic baggies with rubber duckies floating in them or grilled octopus millefeuille. But even though it's billed as Asian-modern fusion, they will appeal to the less adventurous with mains like glazed short ribs or Fish, Chips and More Chips. **Known for:** interesting shareables and killer craft cocktails; excellent sushi and raw bar; a la carte Boozy Brunch all-day Saturday and Sunday. $ *Average main: $40* ⊠ *J. E. Irausquin Blvd. 374, Noord* ☎ *297/280–2463* ⊕ *www.bruttorestaurant.com* ⊙ *No lunch Mon.–Sat.*

Campeones Cantina and Tequila Bar

$$$ | **MEXICAN** | **FAMILY** | The legendary Champions Sports Bar has been totally reimagined into a replica of a colorful Mexican village square with a bar that features 100 different kinds of tequila, premium mescal, and killer margaritas. Endless complimentary nachos, salsa, and fixings are available out of the trunk of a vintage Volkswagen, and the menu, though limited, offers up creative versions of many well-known authentic Mexican specialties. **Known for:** giant burrito to share and freshly prepared Mexican street food; a hot sauce wall with over 30 varieties; lively DJ-driven or live mariachi music. $ *Average main: $22* ⊠ *Marriott's Aruba Ocean Club, L.G. Smith Blvd 99, Palm Beach* ☎ *297/520–6943* ⊕ *www.facebook.com/campeonescantina* ⊙ *No lunch.*

★ Casa Nonna

$$$$ | **ITALIAN** | The cheery Ritz-Carlton breakfast spot known as Solanio takes on a whole new identity in the evenings as it transforms into Casa Nonna (meaning "grandmother's house"), dedicated to serving up authentic Italian cuisine. Service is exquisite (they even have a cocktail cart), and you can taste the care put into the handmade pastas and sauces. **Known for:** authentic house-made pastas and sauces; Mediterranean comfort food, sometimes with a fusion twist; good selection of gluten-free options. $ *Average main: $40* ⊠ *The Ritz-Carlton, Aruba, L. G. Smith Blvd. 107, Noord* ☎ *297/527–2222* ⊕ *www.casanonna.com* ⊙ *Closed Tues. and Thurs.*

★ Da Vinci Ristorante

$$$$ | ITALIAN | FAMILY | Don't let the rustic decor fool you: this is not your average Italian resort eatery, though it's an inviting choice for large groups. Da Vinci pulls out all the stops to present a seriously upscale, authentic, and creative menu of Mediterranean favorites. **Known for:** creative Italian fare; excellent wine cellar; family-friendly yet upscale atmosphere. ⑤ *Average main: $35* ✉ *Holiday Inn Resort Aruba, J. E. Irausquin Blvd. 230, Palm Beach* ☎ 297/586–3600 ⊕ *www.holidayarubaresort.com/en/dining/da-vinci-ristorante/* ۞ *Closed Sun.*

★ Fireson Brewing Company

$$ | INTERNATIONAL | If you're seeking something more pubby than clubby, sleuth out this casual and comforting spot tucked away on The Cove Mall's far corner, facing the Holiday Inn parking lot. It's all about the beer and the bites here, as Fireson offers up their own craft beer and authentic Aruban comfort food like *funchi* fries with cheese, croquettes, and empanadas (*pastechi's* close cousin). **Known for:** excellent craft beer; comfort-food pub fare; shareable plates for four to six people. ⑤ *Average main: $12* ✉ *J. E. Irausquin Blvd 230, Palm Beach* ☎ 297/565–8209 ⊕ *www.firesonbrewing.com* ۞ *Closed Tues. No lunch.*

★ Hanasaki Fusion

$$$ | FUSION | This gorgeously decorated emporium near the Old Windmill is awash in cherry blossoms and soft neon with ultra-modern accents and an exciting inviting feel, but the biggest surprise is the fusion of cuisines all under the same little roof. The menu features a mix of elegantly presented Japanese and Peruvian fare, with excellent sushi renditions as well. **Known for:** stunning decor; trendy creative cocktails; fresh preparations of ceviche and sushi. ⑤ *Average main: $25* ✉ *De Olde Molen Mall, J.E. Irausquin Blvd. 330, Palm Beach* ✛ *Next to Courtyard Aruba Resort* ☎ 297/730-2244 ⊕ *hanasaki-fusion.com* ۞ *No lunch.*

Hostaria Da' Vittorio

$$$ | ITALIAN | FAMILY | At one of Aruba's most legendary Italian eateries, part of the fun is watching chef Vittorio Muscariello prepare authentic Italian regional specialties in his open kitchen. The staff helps you choose wines from the extensive list and recommends portions of hot and cold antipasti, risottos, and pastas. **Known for:** authentic brick-oven pizza; beautiful courtyard dining space; good for large groups. ⑤ *Average main: $30* ✉ *L. G. Smith Blvd. 380, Palm Beach* ☎ 297/586–3838 ⊕ *hostariavittorio.com.*

★ The Journey

$$$$ | INTERNATIONAL | One of the latest dining emporiums to rejuvenate the old windmill quarter, this intimate chef's table experience revolves around the well-known culinary skills and

creativity of Chef Patrick van der Donk and his talented sommelier wife, Ivette. This dynamic duo has a legacy of operating fine
dining establishments on Aruba under the Amuse brand, and now
they invite guests into their latest venture. **Known for:** five-course
chef's choice pre-fixe menu with or without wine pairing; classic
French-inspired cuisine with a Caribbean twist; stellar personal
service. ⑤ *Average main: $120* ⊠ *L. G. Smith Blvd 330, Noord*
✛ *Beside the big red windmill* ☎ *297/565–0535* ⊕ *thejourneyaru-
ba.com* ☾ *Closed weekends. No lunch.*

★ King Fred & Princess Diana

$$ | INTERNATIONAL | The historic 200-year-old red windmill called
De Olde Molen is a famous Aruba landmark, brought from Holland
in 1960 piece by piece and then reconstructed to its original glory.
It has housed many different venues for dining and imbibing over
the years, but now it splits its time as Diana's Pancakes, which
serves up Dutch-style crepes in a variety of delicious styles
during the day, and at night Chef Fred creates an eclectic choice
of international dishes. **Known for:** Dutch-style pancakes by day;
eclectic choice of international dishes by night; fabulous alfresco
bar on top deck of the windmill. ⑤ *Average main: $20* ⊠ *Old Dutch
Windmill, J. E. Irausquin Blvd. 330, Palm Beach* ☎ *297/280–7820*
⊕ *www.kfpdaruba.com* ☾ *Closed Mon. and Tues.*

The Lazy Turtle

$$$ | INTERNATIONAL | This sprawling spot that takes over one entire
side of Paseo Herencia's interior courtyard is anything but lazy;
it's a rollicking affair offering up an eclectic mix of interesting specialties like Cambodian chicken served alongside pastas, steaks,
and seafood with fabulous soups like pumpkin with cashews or
coconut-plantain. The revelry spills over to their new neon-pink
Flamingo's Cocktail Bar across from their outdoor patio, with
its own brand of zany nightlife offerings, creative libations, and
snacks. **Known for:** lively gathering spot; fun friendly staff and creative cocktails; surprising selection of creative vegetarian fare that
can also be made vegan. ⑤ *Average main: $25* ⊠ *Paseo Herencia
Mall, J. E. Irausquin Blvd. 382A, Palm Beach* ☎ *297/587-1992*
⊕ *thelazyturtlearuba.com.*

Madame Janette

$$$$ | INTERNATIONAL | The food at this rustic alfresco garden
restaurant, named after the Scotch bonnet pepper called Madame
Janette in Aruba, is surprisingly French-inspired with a classically
trained chef. Though some dishes are infused with Caribbean flavors, especially fish and seafood, you'll find a lot of classic French
sauces served with the meats; their claim to fame in the past
few years has been the quality of their beef, thanks to their own

The 200-year-old Old Dutch Windmill is home to the King Fred & Princess Diana restaurant.

dry-aging chamber. **Known for:** signature dry-aged steak dinners for two; craft beers and even a beer sommelier; specials that focus on local seasonal ingredients. $ *Average main: $60* ⊠ *Cunucu Abao 37, Cunucu Abao* ☎ *297/587–0184* ⊕ *madamejanette.info* ⊘ *Closed Sun. No lunch.*

MooMba Beach Bar and Restaurant
$$$ | **INTERNATIONAL** | Best known as a beach party spot, this legendary hangout has good food and is a popular place for a seafront breakfast. Dinner under the giant palapa or on the beach is first-rate, as is lunch—particularly since it's the perfect place for people-watching along Aruba's busiest stretch of sand. **Known for:** daily all-you-can-eat prix-fixe breakfast buffet; variety of giant pinchos (skewered meats); sizzling fajitas. $ *Average main: $30* ⊠ *J. E. Irausquin Blvd. 230, Palm Beach* ☎ *297/586–5365* ⊕ *moombabeach.com.*

Old Cunucu House
$$$ | **CARIBBEAN** | Since the mid-1990s executive chef Ligia Maria has delighted diners with delicious and authentic *crioyo* (local) cuisine in a rustic and cozy traditional *cunucu* (countryside) house. Try the house version of Aruba's famous *keshi yena*—chicken, raisins, olives, cashews, peppers, and rice in a hollowed-out Gouda rind— or thick hearty *stobas* (stews) of goat or beef. **Known for:** secret family recipes of traditional Aruban cuisine; hearty portions and good prices; family-run and family-friendly atmosphere. $ *Average main: $25* ⊠ *Palm Beach 150, Palm Beach* ☎ *297/586–1666* ⊕ *www.oldcunucu.com.*

Papiamento

$$$$ | **ECLECTIC** | The Ellis family converted its 126-year-old manor into a bistro with an atmosphere that is elegant, intimate, and always romantic. You can feast in the small dining room, which is filled with antiques, or outdoors on the terrace by the pool. **Known for:** fresh locally sourced ingredients, often from the owner's garden; one of the best places to try keshi yena, Aruba's national dish; large selection of vintages from their Wine Vault. $ *Average main: $35* ✉ *Washington 61, Noord* ☎ *297/586–4544* ⊕ *papiamentoaruba.com* ☾ *Closed Sun. No lunch.*

★ Papillon

$$$$ | **FRENCH** | Inspired by the 1974 Steve McQueen film *Papillon*, evident in the decor, the French- and Caribbean-inspired menu includes classics like frog's legs, escargots, caviar, duck breast with passion-fruit sauce, and local snapper with grilled shrimp covered in creole sauce. Service is old-school stellar, and soft live music adds to the enchanting ambiance. **Known for:** creative vegan recreations of classic French dishes; on- and off-property pop-up chef's table nights; special early-bird prix-fixe menu from 5–7 pm. $ *Average main: $35* ✉ *J. E. Irausquin Blvd. 348A, Palm Beach* ☎ *297/699–5400* ⊕ *papillonaruba.com* ☾ *No lunch.*

★ pureocean

$$$$ | **CONTEMPORARY** | Unfettered sea views and stellar sunsets with tiki lights and lit-up palms make this the signature dining spot of Divi Aruba Phoenix. The menu offers Continental favorites with a Caribbean twist, and guests can enjoy fish, steak, and seafood beachside in the bistro or mere steps from the sea. **Known for:** romantic seaside dinners; a wide selection of international fare; live music Friday and Sunday. $ *Average main: $40* ✉ *Divi Aruba Phoenix Beach Resort, J. E. Irausquin Blvd. 93, Palm Beach* ☎ *297/586–6066 Ext. 7002* ⊕ *www.pureoceanrestaurant.com* ☾ *Closed Tues. and Wed.*

★ Quinta del Carmen

$$$$ | **DUTCH** | Set in a beautifully restored 100-year-old mansion with a lovely outdoor courtyard, Quinta del Carmen's cuisine is best defined as modern Caribbean-Dutch. There are a few traditional Dutch favorites like cheese croquettes and mushrooms and cream; the watermelon salad is sweet, salty, and perfectly refreshing; and the *sucade-lappen* (flank steak stewed in red wine and herbs) has a depth of flavor that comes from hours in the pot. **Known for:** upscale Dutch comfort food; Tapas Garden for shareables; gorgeous antique mansion setting full of avant-garde art. $ *Average main: $35* ✉ *Bubali 119, Noord* ☎ *297/587–7200* ⊕ *quintadelcarmen.com* ☾ *No lunch.*

Rotisserie La Braise

$$ | EUROPEAN | What started as a classic French restaurant has splintered into three distinct alfresco sections—French, Greek, and Italian—with separate menus and separate chefs but still under the same roof. So whether you're in the mood for frog's legs, moussaka, or pasta, this is the spot—plus there are wines from all three regions, too. **Known for:** eclectic choices of cuisine under one roof; rotisserie chicken to-go; excellent French, Italian, and Greek authentic specialties. ⑤ *Average main: $20* ⊠ *The Cove Mall, J. E. Irausquin Blvd. 384A, Palm Beach* ☎ *297/280–0300* ⊕ *facebook.com/rotisserielabraise* ⊗ *No lunch.*

Ruinas del Mar

$$$$ | CARIBBEAN | Built around the concept of the Bushiribana gold mill ruins (the name means "ruins by the sea"), the Hyatt's signature restaurant offers up seafood specialties prepared with a fusion of Caribbean and Mediterranean flavors as well as excellent steaks and freshly prepared Italian dishes. This enchanting oasis is the consummate romantic setting, with a koi lagoon, waterfalls, and a rooftop bougainvillea garden; indoor and outdoor dining is available. **Known for:** romantic setting for date night; Caribbean red snapper with choice of sauces; porterhouse-for-two is a popular couple's choice. ⑤ *Average main: $50* ⊠ *Hyatt Regency Aruba Resort Spa and Casino, J. E. Irausquin Blvd. 85, Palm Beach* ☎ *297/586–1234 ext. 36* ⊕ *www.hyatt.com/en-US/hotel/aruba/ hyatt-regency-aruba-resort-spa-and-casino/aruba/dining* ⊗ *No lunch.*

Ruth's Chris Steak House

$$$$ | AMERICAN | This American steak house chain has been a popular fixture of the Aruba Marriott for years and continues to draw locals and visitors in droves. It is a no-nonsense carnivore's delight with a focus on top-quality steak; those looking for something else will find a few interesting seafood specialties, like barbecue shrimp and sizzling blue crab cakes. **Known for:** top-quality USDA Prime beef; famous dipping trio for steaks: black truffle butter, shiitake demi-glace, and honey-soy glaze; porterhouse for two. ⑤ *Average main: $45* ⊠ *Aruba Marriott Resort and Stellaris Casino, L. G. Smith Blvd. 101, Palm Beach* ☎ *297/520–6600* ⊕ *ruthschris. com/aruba/* ⊗ *No lunch.*

★ Senses Fine Dining

$$$$ | INTERNATIONAL | After a very successful run on Eagle Beach, dynamic duo Chef Kelt Hugo Maat and his partner, sommelier/ host Sebastian Kruisselbrink, decided to relocate their Senses Fine Dining chef's table experience to Palm Beach—but with a twist. Now operating as the signature dining spot of the Radisson

Blu Aruba, this new concept encompasses a dual space that includes the chef's table in a dedicated walled-off corner and a classy a la carte restaurant that is open for lunch and dinner. **Known for:** creative prix-fixe chef's choice dining experiences; the only luxury brunch chef's table in Aruba; upscale shareables like oysters and Champagne. ⑤ *Average main: $45 ⊠ Radisson Blu Aruba, J. E. Irausquin Blvd 97A, Noord* ☎ *297/738–5655* ⊕ *sensesaruba.restaurant.*

Sunset Grille

$$$$ | INTERNATIONAL | Simple and elegant, without a lot of extra gimmicks, this is a no-nonsense modern steak and seafood spot with a focus on fresh and locally sourced ingredients whenever possible. Though there's air-conditioned seating inside, grab a seat outside for dinner to find out why this is called the Sunset Grille. **Known for:** sunset surf-and-turf; prix-fixe Argentinian charcoal grill dinners for two; Aruban seafood risotto. ⑤ *Average main: $45 ⊠ Hilton Aruba Caribbean Resort and Casino, J. E. Irausquin Blvd. 81, Noord* ☎ *297/526–6612* ⊕ *hiltonaruba.com/dining/.*

2 Fools and a Bull Gourmet Studio

$$$$ | INTERNATIONAL | One of Aruba's very first forays into the chef's table experience, here you'll enjoy an intimate evening of culinary entertainment that plays like a fun dinner party with friends rather than something you pay for. At most, 17 guests are assembled around the U-shaped communal dinner table for a 5-and-a-half course creative gourmet adventure. **Known for:** an intimate chef's table experience; perfect wine pairings (optional); adults-only with reservations required far in advance. ⑤ *Average main: $130 ⊠ Palm Beach 17, Noord* ☎ *297/586–7177* ⊕ *www. aruba.2foolsandabull.com.*

★ The Vue Rooftop Restaurant and Bar

$$$$ | INTERNATIONAL | The crowning glory of all the options at The Cove Mall is this aptly named second-story bar and restaurant where a private elevator introduces guests to incredible vistas at any time of day. But it's not so much the view that draws the crowds here as it is the vibe—think private beach cabanas with killer mixologists behind the bar, and romantic tables for two scattered around a rooftop—and the food, which ranges from creative tapas and shareables like seafood towers and charcuterie boards to upscale mains like steak, lamb chops, lobster, and fresh fish. **Known for:** exclusive VIP cabana rentals with luxe amenties; trendy hot spot for the "beautiful people"; exquisite handcrafted cocktails. ⑤ *Average main: $45 ⊠ The Cove Mall, J. E. Irausquin Blvd. 384A, Palm Beach* ☎ *297/280–0279* ⊕ *thevuerooftoparuba. com* ⊗ *No lunch.*

Coffee and Quick Bites

Drunk's Denial

$$ | **INTERNATIONAL** | Look for the giant black-and-white-striped booth in the interior courtyard of Paseo Herencia for some truly decadent delights. Specializing in alcohol-infused gourmet baked goods, particularly little Bundt cakes (no cupcakes here) that are infused with your choice of liquor-laden syrups, there are also specialty coffees, sweet or savory crêpes, waffle bowls, ice cream, and frozen yogurt, all available with "drunken toppings." **Known for:** delicious and unique customizable baked treats; cakes-to-go that are ideal customizable gifts for special occasions; artisanal homemade drunken syrups like tequila honey or rum chocolate fudge. ⑤ *Average main: $11* ⊠ *Paseo Herencia Mall, J. E. Irausquin Blvd. 382A, Palm Beach* ☎ *297/594–3222* ⊕ *drunksdenial.com.*

Eduardo's Beach Shack

$ | **INTERNATIONAL** | This cheery little hut on Palm Beach is famous for its healthy and delicious fresh fruit and veggie juices, smoothies, bowls, kombucha, and creative vegan options. All of their specialties are free of additives and artificial substances. **Known for:** fresh, healthy, and delicious fare; soft-serve dairy-free ice cream; large selection of healthy bowls and smoothies. ⑤ *Average main: $11* ⊠ *J. E. Irausquin Blvd. 87, Noord* ✛ *In front of Playa Linda Resort* ☎ *297/699-9823* ⊕ *eduardosbeachshack.com* ☉ *No dinner.*

Scott's Brats

$$ | **INTERNATIONAL** | These expat American owners brought a taste of home to their alfresco Palm Beach bar hut with authentic Wisconsin brats and sausages, Chicago-style hot dogs, and their great selection of loaded fries. They also have funnel cakes, coffee, and some killer creative cocktails. **Known for:** sandwiches and rolls stuffed with meat; ribs, chicken, sausages, and tacos; "Funky Fries" menu with weird yet tasty toppings. ⑤ *Average main: $12* ⊠ *J. E. Irausquin Blvd. 87, Palm Beach* ☎ *297/593–6940* ⊕ *www. facebook.com/scottsbrats.*

🛏 Hotels

Aruba Marriott Resort and Stellaris Casino

$$$$ | **RESORT** | **FAMILY** | This full-service resort offers both family-friendly amenities as well as an adults-only exclusive floor that has its own pool and snazzy lounge on the ground floor. **Pros:** lots of water sport options right out front; adults-only oasis and adults-only floor; one of the island's best casinos. **Cons:** main pool can be noisy and crowded with kids; not all rooms have sea views; beachfront can become crowded in high season. ⑤ *Rooms*

The Aruba Marriott Resort & Stellaris Casino is in the heart of Palm Beach.

from: $605 ✉ *L. G. Smith Blvd. 101, Palm Beach* ☎ *297/586–9000,
800/223–6388* ⊕ *arubamarriott.com* ↪ *414 rooms* ❧ *No Meals.*

Barceló Aruba
$$ | RESORT | FAMILY | This family-friendly all-inclusive offers some-
thing for everyone, with an extensive pool complex, great nightly
entertainment, a dedicated kids' club, and an eclectic choice of a
la carte dining. **Pros:** spacious rooms, many with good sea views;
excellent location for Palm Beach water sports and shopping; Royal Club level has a dedicated dining room and lounge. **Cons:** beach
in front can get very crowded; pool area can be very noisy with
activities; most rooms have partial sea views. ⑤ *Rooms from:
$350* ✉ *J. E. Irausquin Blvd. 83, Palm Beach* ☎ *297/586–4500*
⊕ *barcelo.com/en-us/barcelo-aruba/* ↪ *373 rooms* ❧ *All-Inclusive.*

★ Boardwalk Boutique Hotel Aruba
$$$ | HOTEL | What began as a tiny family-run enclave on a historic
coconut plantation has since evolved into an enchanting boutique
resort of Caribbean cottage-style *casitas* connected by a signature
wooden boardwalk and surrounded in vibrant blooms. **Pros:** stellar
personal service and health and wellness focus; modern digital
amenities like key and concierge apps and 5G Wi-Fi; new on-site
Coco Café offers full breakfast, all-day lunch, and bar options.
Cons: not right on the beach; little on-site entertainment; smokers
must indulge outside of the property's security gates. ⑤ *Rooms
from: $450* ✉ *Bakval 20, Palm Beach* ☎ *297/586–6654* ⊕ *www.
boardwalkaruba.com* ↪ *46 units* ❧ *No Meals* ☞ *Credit cards
only, no cash.*

Courtyard Aruba Resort by Marriott

$$ | HOTEL | A bright, contemporary economical alternative to the high-rises on Palm Beach, this property is ideally suited for work-cations or small group getaways, with modern rooms outfitted with the latest technology and an inviting pool area that includes a swim-up bar and a small spa on-site. **Pros:** clean modern rooms; great value; walking distance to the beach. **Cons:** not right on the sea; little entertainment; beach chairs do not include shade palapas. *Rooms from: $300* ⊠ *J. E. Irausquin Blvd. 330, Palm Beach* ☎ *297/586–7700* ⊕ *marriott.com/en-us/hotels/auacy-courtyard-aruba-resort* ⤶ *192 rooms* ⦾ *No Meals.*

★ Divi Aruba Phoenix Beach Resort

$$$$ | RESORT | FAMILY | With incredible views from its high-rise tower, stunning rooms awash in tropical colors, state-of-the-art amenities, and comfortable homey accommodations, Divi Aruba Phoenix rises above the fray on busy Palm Beach. **Pros:** beautifully appointed rooms, some with whirlpool bathtubs; great private beach away from the main Palm Beach frenzy; all units have sea views. **Cons:** no shuttle service to other Divi properties; no all-inclusive plan; no reserving shade palapas. *Rooms from: $740* ⊠ *J. E. Irausquin Blvd. 75, Palm Beach* ☎ *297/586–6066* ⊕ *www.diviarubaphoenix.com* ⤶ *240 rooms* ⦾ *No Meals.*

Hilton Aruba Caribbean Resort and Casino

$$$$ | HOTEL | FAMILY | Sprawling over 15 acres of white sand and lush tropical gardens with a lovely waterfall winding throughout, this iconic resort was the first to debut on Palm Beach in 1959 and was the birthplace of the famous Aruba Ariba cocktail. **Pros:** excellent beachfront area never feels crowded, even when at capacity; grand ballroom is ideal for big events; Palm Beach Club has special perks and a lounge. **Cons:** not all rooms have sea views; sometimes long lines at the breakfast buffets; food and drink can be pricey. *Rooms from: $649* ⊠ *J. E. Irausquin Blvd. 81, Palm Beach* ☎ *297/586–6555* ⊕ *hiltonaruba.com* ⤶ *357 rooms* ⦾ *No Meals.*

★ Holiday Inn Resort Aruba

$$$ | RESORT | FAMILY | This resort's massive lemon-yellow buildings that sprawl across a pristine stretch of Palm Beach offer a revelation compared to what most might think a Holiday Inn stay might entail—inviting rooms, a fun vibe, and distinct sections that will appeal to those looking for quiet active fun or a family-friendly environment. **Pros:** a new small, modern on-site casino adds to the entertainment options; kids stay free and enjoy an excellent kids' club; right across the street from the best Palm Beach nightlife. **Cons:** not all rooms have sea views; shade palapas need

to be reserved and rented; reception can be busy with big groups. ⑤ *Rooms from: $415* ✉ *J. E. Irausquin Blvd. 230, Palm Beach* ☎ *297/586–3600, 800/465–4329* ⊕ *www.holidayarubaresort.com* ⇱ *590 rooms* ⦿ *No Meals.*

Hotel Riu Palace Antillas

$$$$ | **RESORT** | Right next door to Hotel Riu Palace Aruba, its family-friendly sister, this high-rise tower is strictly for adults, offering all-inclusive rates and a fabulous pool area right on the beach where they hold their famous RIU brand theme parties. **Pros:** full bottles of standard spirits, beer, and soft drinks in all rooms; arguably the best and biggest all-inclusive buffet on the island; 24/7 room service included. **Cons:** rooms are small by modern standards; common areas appear more corporate than resort-tropical; construction of new St. Regis hotel next door will obstruct many sea view rooms. ⑤ *Rooms from: $630* ✉ *J. E. Irausquin Blvd. 77, Palm Beach* ☎ *297/526–4100* ⊕ *www.riu.com* ⇱ *482 rooms* ⦿ *All-Inclusive.*

Hotel Riu Palace Aruba

$$$$ | **RESORT** | **FAMILY** | This family-friendly all-inclusive is a massive complex surrounding an expansive beachfront water circuit with a choice of five restaurants and scads of free activities. **Pros:** spacious water circuit for families; a wide choice of entertainment and dining; nice shallow beachfront. **Cons:** beach and pool area get very busy and noisy; few spots to escape in solitude; few rooms have unobstructed sea views. ⑤ *Rooms from: $656* ✉ *J. E. Irausquin Blvd. 79, Palm Beach* ☎ *297/586–3900* ⊕ *www.riu.com/en/hotel/aruba/palmbeach/hotel-riu-palace-aruba/* ⇱ *450 rooms* ⦿ *All-Inclusive.*

Hyatt Regency Aruba Resort, Spa, and Casino

$$$$ | **RESORT** | **FAMILY** | Located on 12 acres of prime beachfront, the resort delivers an intimate island escape in the heart of Palm Beach. **Pros:** luxurious adults-only beachfront pool; lush tropical landscaping leads down to spacious beachfront; many rooms have spectacular ocean views. **Cons:** few rooms have full balconies; some standard rooms are on the small side with small balconies; not all rooms have sea views. ⑤ *Rooms from: $599* ✉ *J. E. Irausquin Blvd. 85, Palm Beach* ☎ *297/586–1234, 800/554–9288* ⊕ *www.hyatt.com/en-US/hotel/aruba/hyatt-regency-aruba-resort-spa-and-casino/aruba* ⇱ *359 rooms* ⦿ *No Meals.*

Marriott's Aruba Ocean Club

$$$$ | **TIMESHARE** | **FAMILY** | First-rate amenities and contemporarily decorated villas with balconies and full kitchens have made this property an island favorite. **Pros:** relaxed atmosphere; feels more like a home than a hotel room; excellent beach. **Cons:** beach can get crowded; attracts large families, so lots of kids are about; grounds are not within view of the sea. $ *Rooms from: $875* ✉ *L. G. Smith Blvd. 99, Palm Beach* ☎ *297/586–9000* ⊕ *www.marriott. com/en-us/hotels/auaao-marriotts-aruba-ocean-club/overview/* ⤴ *311 suites* ¶⊘ *No Meals.*

Playa Linda Beach Resort
$$$$ | TIMESHARE | FAMILY | Looking something like a stepped Mayan pyramid—the design maximizes sea views from the balconies—this older timeshare hotel also has a homey feel, with full kitchens in all the spacious units. **Pros:** great beach location; spacious rooms and townhomes; lots of distractions for the kids. **Cons:** not all rooms are of the same standard; can be a crowded and busy beachfront; not all rooms have sea views. $ *Rooms from: $602* ✉ *J. E. Irausquin Blvd. 87, Palm Beach* ☎ *297/586–1000* ⊕ *playalinda.com* ⤴ *144 rooms, 3 townhomes* ¶⊘ *No Meals.*

★ Radisson Blu Aruba
$$$ | HOTEL | FAMILY | This stylish modern high-rise behind the Palm Beach strip overlooks a gorgeous water circuit right across the street from all the shopping and dazzling nightlife. **Pros:** ideal for families that want space; the only LEED-certified green resort in Aruba; expansive water circuit includes an adults-only pool and a whirlpool nook. **Cons:** not all rooms have sea views; not all rooms have balconies; not on the beach. $ *Rooms from: $400* ✉ *J. E. Irausquin Blvd. 97A, Noord* ☎ *866/856–9066* ⊕ *www.radissonhotelsamericas.com/en-us/hotels/radisson-blu-aruba* ⤴ *132 rooms* ¶⊘ *No Meals.*

★ The Ritz-Carlton, Aruba
$$$$ | HOTEL | All of the rooms and suites and many common areas at this massive beachfront hotel were completely refreshed in 2023 to reflect Aruban island life with cactus art and soothing sea and sand tones, and all accommodations have oversize bathtubs and luxury products. **Pros:** exemplary personal service; spacious grounds so it never feels crowded; stunning sunset views from rooms and the atrium lobby bar. **Cons:** sheer size and design gives it a big-box feel; attracts many large groups; pricey compared to other similar properties. $ *Rooms from: $750* ✉ *L. G. Smith Blvd. 107, Palm Beach* ☎ *297/527–2222* ⊕ *www.ritzcarlton.com/en/hotels/auart-the-ritz-carlton-aruba/overview/* ⤴ *320 rooms* ¶⊘ *No Meals.*

🍸 Nightlife

The 2-mile stretch of road in front of the high-rise resorts called "The Strip" is where you'll find most of the nightlife action in Palm Beach, and The Cove Mall has become an anchor of hot spots. The clubs tend to come and go, but this area's squares, courtyards, and outdoor malls are always chock-full of opportunities to let loose after the sun goes down. Threaded throughout are vendor kiosks, too. You can easily barhop or casino-hop on foot to find the vibe that suits you best—just follow the music that moves you. If you're staying in a Palm Beach resort, there's no need for a car or taxi.

★ Bugaloe Beach Bar and Grill

BARS | Night and day, this crazy colorful beach bar at the tip of De Palm Pier on busy Palm Beach is packed. Paint-spattered wooden tables and chairs on a plank floor under a massive palapa draw barefoot beachcombers in for frozen cocktails, cold beer, and casual fare where live music is king. There are karaoke nights, salsa nights, and daily food specials including breakfast. It's an optimal spot to catch a magical sunset over the waves. ⊠ *De Palm Pier, J. E. Irausquin Blvd. 79, Palm Beach* ☎ *297/586–2233* ⊕ *bugaloe.com.*

The Bulldog Aruba

BARS | Based on the famous Bulldog in the Netherlands, this one is all about partying hearty in the center of Paseo Herencia's courtyard with zany antics by the barkeeps and lots of dance action after the water shows end. ⊠ *Paseo Herencia Mall, J. E. Irausquin Blvd. 382A, Palm Beach* ☎ *297/563–7951* ⊕ *www.facebook.com/ thebulldogaruba.*

★ Craft and Lola

GATHERING PLACES | These odd-combination sister spots are hard to miss on the Palm Beach strip with their colorful outdoor decor. They share a wide swath of the sidewalk, but they specialize in two very different things. Craft is best known as a quality coffee bar and breakfast spot; they serve breakfast until 4 pm with a legendary Saturday Live Music Brunch and Boogie Nights every Saturday that start at 10 pm. Lola, next door, is all about casual Mexican fare and margaritas at lunch, but turns into a full-on fiesta place late night. It's a strange fusion of offerings but it works, and both spots are typically hopping, so make reservations—especially for dinner at Lola. ⊠ *J. E. Irausquin Blvd. 348A, Palm Beach* ☎ *297/743–9522* ⊕ *www.craftaruba.com; www.lolataqueria.com.*

The Lobby

GATHERING PLACES | Located in the spacious lobby of the Aruba Marriott Resort and Stellaris Casino, this cool and classy enclave is also about craft cocktails, sushi rolls, sips, snacks, and sometimes soft live lounge music. The combination provides an escape ideal for pre-dinner or post-partying relaxation. Don't miss their unique Aruba Mule cocktail, made with aloe vera juice. ⊠ *Aruba Marriott Resort and Stellaris Casino, L. G. Smith Blvd. 101, Palm Beach* ☎ *297/520–6580* ⊕ *www.marriott.com/en-us/hotels/auaar-aruba-marriott-resort-and-stellaris-casino/dining/.*

Local Store

BARS | Contrary to its name, it's not a store but a bar, and a very local one at that. Live local bands, lots of resident partiers, and a laid-back, down-to-earth atmosphere make this the place to kick back and have fun, especially on weekends. Good prices on drinks, a huge selection of craft beers, local Aruban snacks like *funchi* fries (made from seasoned cornmeal or polenta with a crispy outside and a creamy inside), and over a dozen kinds of artisanal chicken wings attract the tourists, too. ⊠ *Palm Beach 13A, Noord* ☎ *297/586–1414* ⊕ *www.localstorearuba.com.*

★ MooMba Beach Bar & Restaurant

GATHERING PLACES | As the central party spot on the busiest part of Palm Beach, this open-air bar is famous for its Sunday-night blowouts with big crowds of locals gathering to dance in the sand to live bands or DJs. The barkeeps are mixology masters, and happy hours are very popular. Check their website for current and upcoming special events. The attached restaurant is also a wonderful surf-side spot for breakfast (big buffet until noon), lunch, and dinner, and there are tables in the sand for romantic dinners before partying. You can also rent lounges and umbrellas on the beach and order from their bar menu. ⊠ *J. E. Irausquin Blvd. 230, Palm Beach* ⊹ *Between Holiday Inn and Marriott Surf Club* ☎ *297/586–5365* ⊕ *www.moombabeach.com.*

The Office Aruba

DANCE CLUBS | The island's coolest new dance hot spot has great DJs and dazzling techno light shows that welcome people to party late into the night in the same complex as Brutto Beach Bar just off the Strip. It's a great excuse to put on your glam to enjoy stellar craft cocktails and dance 'till you drop, and it's one of the few spots on Aruba with VIP tables and bottle service. Check their Facebook page for the music schedule and specials. ⊠ *J. E. Irausquin Blvd. 374, Noord* ☎ *297/569–7559* ⊕ *www.theofficearuba.com* ☾ *Closed Sun.–Thurs.*

★ purebeach

BARS | A very lively happy-hour spot with its cool swim-up pool bar, purebeach is the place to be, especially on Sundays for live music and dancing. They are also open for breakfast, lunch, and dinner, but day or night, they are known for killer Caribbean cocktails and creative international fare with weekly specials. There's also an oversize adult-only seafront whirlpool right beside it for romantic nights under the tropical stars with music. Steps from the sea, there are beachfront tables that are a great place to enjoy happy hour (5–6 pm) while watching the sunset. ⊠ *Divi Phoenix Aruba Resort, J. E. Irausquin Blvd. 75, Palm Beach* ☎ *297/586–6066 ext. 7002* ⊕ *purebeacharuba.com.*

★ The Sopranos Piano Bar

PIANO BARS | This lively piano bar is loosely based on the old Sopranos television series decor-wise. Nightly live music with showstopping talent encourages the crowd to join in sing-alongs. Visitors are invited to take the mic, which they've been known to do. Top-notch barkeeps shake up a big list of creative cocktails, and the top-shelf spirit list is impressive. It's loud and rowdy most nights, but nostalgic and low-key when there are no crowds. ⊠ *Arawak Garden Mall, L. G. Smith Blvd. 177, Palm Beach* ☎ *297/586–8622* ⊕ *www.sopranospianobararuba.com.*

 Performing Arts

Caribbean Cinemas VIP

FILM | FAMILY | Ideal for the rare rainy day, or just for something different than the beach, catch a first-run flick in air-conditioned comfort at this ultramodern venue with six stadium-seating auditoriums; the cinema opens daily at 2 pm. The fully reclinable leather seats and lots of space between the rows make it even more inviting for a family outing. ⊠ *Paseo Herencia Mall, J. E. Irausquin Blvd. 382A, Palm Beach* ☎ *297/582–3693.*

🛍 Shopping

GIFTS AND SOUVENIRS
★ The Juggling Fish

JEWELRY & WATCHES | This whimsical shop just off the sand is really two separate entities. One side is Juggling Fish Swimwear, a comprehensive selection of quality bathing suits and beach accessories for the entire family, and the other side is dedicated to a selection of creative and unique gifts and souvenirs, including avant-garde jewelry and handcrafted items. The staff is warm and friendly, and a portion of all proceeds goes to community programs and charities. ⊠ *Playa Linda Beach Resort, Palm Beach* ☎ *297/592-7802* ⊕ *www.thejugglingfish.com.*

★ T. H. Palm & Company

ANTIQUES & COLLECTIBLES | With an eclectic collection of upscale and exclusive items curated from all over the world by the owner, this unique boutique offers everything from top-line fashions for men and women—including footwear, handcrafted jewelry, and accessories—to art deco items for the home and novelty gifts for pets. It's a very popular spot for locals to buy gifts, as well as for visitors to buy one-of-a-kind souvenirs. A portion of all proceeds goes to the community through a special give-back program. ⊠ *J. E. Irausquin Blvd. 87, Palm Beach* ☎ *297/592–7804* ⊕ *www. thpalmandcompany.com.*

JEWELRY

★ Shiva's Gold and Gems

JEWELRY & WATCHES | A reputable family-run business with shops throughout the Caribbean, this Palm Beach Plaza location saves shoppers from heading to Oranjestad for the type of top-quality diamonds and jewelry Downtown is famous for (though there is a location Downtown as well). Luxury watches, precious gems, gold, silver, and more are first-rate here, and this is the only store on Aruba that belongs to the Leading Jewelers of the World, which has fewer than 100 retail members. ⊠ *Palm Beach Plaza Mall, L. G. Smith 95, Palm Beach* ☎ *297/583–4011* ⊕ *www.shivas-jewelers.com* ۞ *Closed Sun.*

MALLS AND MARKETPLACES

Palm Beach Plaza Mall

MALL | FAMILY | This modern, multistory air-conditioned mall offers fashion, tech, electronics, jewelry, souvenirs, and more. Entertainment includes glow-in-the-dark bowling and local festivals and events like fashion shows. Dining includes a food court and stand-alone restaurants like Iguana Joe's. Free Wi-Fi and parking are a bonus, too. ⊠ *L. G. Smith Blvd. 95, Palm Beach* ☎ *297/586–0045* ⊕ *www.facebook.com/PalmBeachPlazaMall.*

★ Paseo Herencia Mall

MALL | FAMILY | A gorgeous, old-fashioned colonial-style courtyard and clock tower encase souvenir and specialty shops, cinemas, dining spots, cafés, and bars. Just off Palm Beach, this low-rise alfresco mall is famous for its nightly "liquid fireworks" shows—neon-lit water fountains waltz to music in a choreographed dance. Visitors can enjoy it for free from an outdoor amphitheater where many cultural events take place, and there's also an Aruban walk of fame and a fancy carousel for children. New dining outlets line the outside street entrances and food truck–style kiosks offer

The Paseo Herencia Mall has a carousel, as well as a nightly "liquid fireworks" show and lots of places to eat and shop.

authentic Aruban snacks. It's an ideal spot for all ages. Late-night shopping with many brand outlets add to the allure. ⊠ *J. E. Irausquin Blvd. 382A, Palm Beach* ☎ *297/586–6533* ⊕ *www. paseoherencia.com.*

PERFUMES AND COSMETICS

★ Maggy's Perfumery and Salon

PERFUME | A true local success story, this is one of the four locations in a local chain that began as a small salon in San Nicolas and evolved into a major perfumery with salons and stores. Though the original Maggy has since passed, the business she began in 1969 is still going strong with her daughter at the helm and many family members still running the business. Quality perfumes and beauty products, as well as health and beauty care services are to be found at all outlets. She also has an online shop now, too. ⊠ *Paseo Herencia Mall, J.E Irausquin Blvd. #382-A, Noord* ☎ *297/529–2118* ⊕ *www.maggysaruba.com.*

Western Tip (California Dunes)

No trip to Aruba is complete without a visit to the California Light-house, and it's also worth exploring the rugged area of the island's Western Tip. The rippling snow-white sand dunes nearby are a wonderful spot for romantic seaside stroll. This is the transition point between Aruba's calmer and rougher coasts. Malmok and

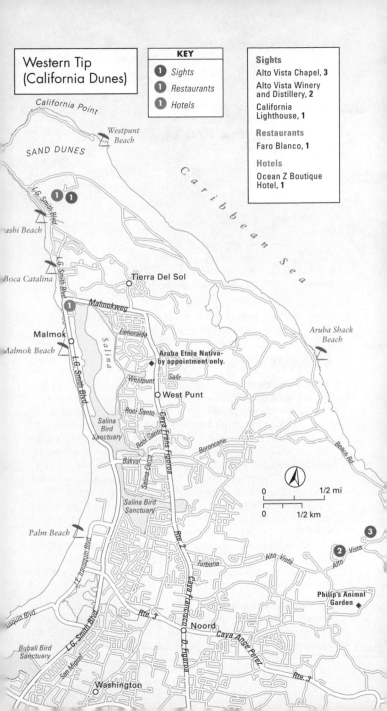

Arashi Beach is a good place to swim and snorkel.

Arashi beaches are popular with locals and excellent spots for grabbing dramatic sunset photos.

Sights

★ Alto Vista Chapel
NOTABLE BUILDING | Meaning "high view," Alto Vista was built in 1750 as the island's first Roman Catholic church. The simple yellow-and-orange structure stands out in bright contrast to its stark desert-like surroundings, and its elevated location offers a wonderful panoramic view of the northwest coast. Restored in 1953, it still holds regular services today and also serves as the culmination point of the annual Walk of the Cross at Easter. You will see small signposts guiding the faithful to the Stations of the Cross all along the winding road to its entrance. This landmark is a typical stop on most island tours. Make sure to walk out back to see the Aruba Peace Labyrinth. ■**TIP→ Make sure to buy coconut water from the famous coconut man out front.** ⊠ *Alto Vista Rd., Noord* ⊹ *Follow the rough, winding dirt road that loops around the island's northern tip or, from the hotel strip, take Palm Beach Rd. through three intersections and watch for the asphalt road to the left.*

Alto Vista Winery and Distillery
WINERY | Aruba's first estate winery opened in 2023 and proved the impossible on such an arid desert island. Guests can tour the vineyard, the distillery, and the winery; do a wine or rum tasting; have some snacks; and hear the whole intriguing story. Tours,

5

which last about an hour and half, are held every Thursday, Friday, and Saturday from 4:30 to 6 pm. Comfortable shoes are encouraged for the tour. ⊠ *Alto Vista, Noord* ⊹ *close to the Alto Vista Chapel* ☎ *297/735–3505* ⊕ *www.altovistawinery.com* ⊠ *$39.*

★ California Lighthouse

LIGHTHOUSE | FAMILY | Built in 1916, the landmark lighthouse on the island's northwestern tip is open to the public, and visitors can climb the spiral stairs to discover a fabulous panoramic view for a small fee. Declared a national monument in 2015, the lighthouse was built because of and named after the merchant ship *California* that sunk nearby. There are also spectacular private catered three-course dinner experiences for two people at the top that can be booked through Experitours; there's a choice of sunset or under-the-stars seating. They also do a catered breakfast. It's one of only two lighthouse dining experiences in the world. ⊠ *2 Hudishibana* ☎ *297/699–0995* ⊕ *www.facebook.com/CaliforniaLighthouseAruba* ⊠ *$5.*

Beaches

★ Arashi Beach

BEACH | This is the local favorite, a half-mile stretch of gleaming white sand with much rougher rolling surf than the other popular beaches and some great snorkeling on the ends. It can get busy on weekends—especially on Sunday—with local families bringing their own picnics, and visitors have discovered a cool little beach bar called Arashi Beach Shack (⊕ www.facebook.com/ ArashiBeachShack) with great food, drinks, a lounge, and beach umbrella rentals. **Amenities:** food and drink; toilets; parking (free). **Best for:** swimming; snorkeling. ⊠ *Malmokweg* ⊹ *West of Malmok Beach, on the west end.*

Boca Catalina

BEACH | A fairly isolated strip off a residential area, this tiny white-sand cove attracts snorkelers with its shallow water filled with fish and cool little caves. Swimmers will also appreciate the calm conditions. There aren't any facilities nearby, just a few public shade palapas but no chairs, so pack provisions and your own snorkel gear. It's popular with locals on weekends. **Amenities:** none. **Best for:** snorkeling; swimming. ⊠ *Malmokweg* ⊹ *Between Arashi Beach and Malmok Beach, north of intersection of Rtes. 1B and 2B* ⊕ *www.aruba.com/us/explore/boca-catalina.*

Malmok Beach (*Boca Catalina*)

BEACH | On the northwestern shore, this small cove bordered by limestone cliffs crests shallow waters that stretch 300 yards from shore. There are no snack or refreshment stands, but that might

change with the addition of the new stretch of paved Linear Park path leading from Fisherman's Huts to Arashi beaches which attracts plenty of cyclists, strollers, and runners. Most of the main snorkel boat tours stop here for a dip, as the water is crystal clear and full of tropical fish, so it can become very crowded after lunch. Go early in the morning if you want to swim/snorkel on your own. Wear beach shoes as the tiny strips of sand where you can gain access to the water are very rocky. You might see sea turtles there. **Amenities:** none. **Best for:** solitude; snorkeling; sunset. ⊠ *J. E. Irausquin Blvd., Malmokweg.*

 # Restaurants

Faro Blanco

$$$$ | **ITALIAN** | Next to the iconic California Lighthouse in the former lighthouse keeper's home, this restaurant is best known for its Italian fare and grand open-air terrace overlooking the rugged West Coast seascape. The menu offers a selection of gourmet pasta, pizza, risottos, fish, seafood, and meats served with classic Italian flair and an extensive wine selection. **Known for:** stunning sunset views from an elevated perch; Italian classics like osso buco; chef's special Caribbean lobster tail with homemade ravioli and brandy sauce. ⑤ *Average main: $45* ⊠ *California Lighthouse* ☎ *297/586–0787* ⊕ *faroblancorestaurant.com.*

 # Hotels

Ocean Z Boutique Hotel

$$$$ | **HOTEL** | A unique luxury boutique resort far from the touristy fray is across the road from the wild and scenic Malmok Cliffs, offering rooms surrounding a solarium pool as well as a few oceanfront suites with their own dipping pools. **Pros:** chic solitary escape away from the crowds; gorgeous scenic setting with sea views; intimate and personal first-rate service. **Cons:** not within walking distance to any other dining or shopping; not on a beach; no entertainment. ⑤ *Rooms from: $563* ⊠ *L. G. Smith Blvd. 526, Malmokweg* ☎ *297/586–9500* ⊕ *oceanzaruba.com* ⤴ *13 rooms.*

 # Shopping

There is little shopping on this far end of the island, beyond small boutiques in the hotels and local convenience stores.

SAN NICOLAS AND SAVANETA

Updated by
Susan Campbell

⊙ Sights   🍴 Restaurants   🛏 Hotels   ● Shopping   🍸 Nightlife

★★★★☆   ★★★★★   ★★★★★   ★★★★★   ★★★★★

NEIGHBORHOOD SNAPSHOT

TOP EXPERIENCES

■ **Take a Mural Walk:** San Nicolas has incredible outdoor art and murals that have rejuvenated the town.

■ **Try a Boozer Colada:** Visit legendary Charlie's Bar and Restaurant for this potent signature cocktail.

■ **Eat the Freshest Seafood:** At Zeerovers in Savaneta, watch fishermen bring in their catch and then pick exactly what you want for lunch.

■ **Relax at Baby Beach:** Go snorkeling to really experience all this beach's wonders.

■ **Stay in an Overwater Bungalow:** Sleuth out the unique and luxurious Aruba Ocean Villas.

■ **Check Out Mangel Halto's Mangrove Canals:** Kayak or paddleboard through the canals' calm waters.

GETTING HERE AND AROUND

There is a public bus from Downtown Oranjestad to Savaneta and San Nicolas, but it takes a long time. Taxis are pricey but worth it, if you're going for dinner and don't want to drink and drive. Or hire a driver for the day to explore the area. From Downtown Oranjestad, it should take about 15 minutes to drive to Savaneta and about 20–25 minutes to get to San Nicolas.

PLANNING YOUR TIME

Sunday's the most popular beach day for locals, and many shops are closed. The best time to visit San Nicolas and Savaneta is during the day, but Savaneta has some great dinner options.

VIEWFINDER

■ The giant red anchor outside of Seroe Colorado honoring the seafarers is a popular photo stop, and the rugged coastline there offers gorgeous natural vistas. You can also capture stunning shots from Rum Reef's infinity pool overlooking breathtaking Baby Beach. But you need not venture any further than San Nicolas proper for a gazillion exceptional Insta-worthy muses as the entire downtown grid is bedecked with outstanding outdoor murals and art. Explore it on your own or take a guided tour with Aruba Mural Tours (⊕arubamuraltours.com), led by the organization that spearheaded the mural movement.

Savaneta, the island's original capital, is historically referred to as Commander's Bay, since this is where the first Dutch commanders resided. Farther south, the little ex-refinery town of San Nicolas is known locally as Sunrise City, due to its brilliant sunrises. Today, both towns are receiving renewed interest as tourist destinations as they begin to focus more on preserving and promoting the island's history, culture, and art.

Planning

Festivals and Street Parties

★ Aruba Art Week

ARTS FESTIVALS | Organized by ArtisA, this annual event takes place each fall when artists from around the world are invited to collaborate on outdoor installations, sculptures, murals, and more throughout San Nicolas. Immersive and interactive events include the Aruba Art Fair, which highlights workshops with the artists; the Youth Art Fair, which showcases the island's young aspiring creators; and the ArtFashion show, which features stunning works of local designers. There are also special events like pop-up restaurants, culinary art competitions, and lots of music and dancing turning downtown into one big festive street party. The work left behind from past years has turned the downtown core into a magical maze of outdoor art and will continue to do so for years to come. ⊠ *San Nicolas Promenade, San Nicolaas* ☎ *297/593–4475* ⊕ *arubaartfair.com.*

Carnival

GATHERING PLACES | Most of the main events during the annual Carnival take place in Oranjestad, but San Nicolas is considered to be the birthplace of the island's Carnival traditions. Celebrations include a lighting parade, music competitions, and a mini-grand parade the day before the big one in Oranjestad. And this is the only location for Jouvert Morning, the annual sunrise road march that starts at 4 am—another reason the town was dubbed "Sunrise City." The new Carnival Village in the heart of town hosts many more events year-round, and on weekend nights you'll often have small bands outside the colorful little food truck–style kiosks for local's night out. You can also grab some great local food and cold beer there during the day after 11 am; there's always at least one of them open. ⊠ *San Nicolas, Aruba, Savaneta* ⊕ *www.aruba. com/us/calendar/grand-carnival-parade-in-san-nicolas.*

Tours

★ Aruba Mural Tours

WALKING TOURS | There's no better way to experience the incredible art revolution that has taken over the San Nicolas streets than with a guided tour. Guests learn the story behind each work, as well as the creator's personal history, and get to experience some interactive elements that are exposed with special gear or apps that the guides provide. Regular tours that last about 2 hours are offered on select mornings and afternoons; transportation to and from San Nicolas can be provided. A full-day tour that also includes sun and fun time at Baby Beach is available, as is a full-day tour and art workshop where you can create your own masterpiece under the tutelage of a well-known local artist. The minimum age for walking tours is 6 and 16 for workshops. ■TIP➜ **The Fin di Luna Tour is half-price on the last Saturday of the month.** ⊠ *Bernard van de Veen Zeppenfeldstraat 6, San Nicolaas* ☎ *297/593–4475* ⊕ *arubamuraltours.com* 🖃 *From $30.*

San Nicolas

During the oil refinery heyday, Aruba's oldest village was a bustling port and the island's economic hub. As demand for oil dwindled and tourism rose, attention shifted to Oranjestad and the island's best beaches. The past few years have seen a renaissance in San Nicolas, largely due to the improvement of its infrastructure and the beautification of its main streets, which have become an exciting outdoor art district. The annual Aruba Art Fair leaves incredible modern outdoor art in its wake each year and attracts many international visitors to its colorful grid of outdoor murals and interactive exhibits.

Today there are also small museums, a retro cinema, a big carnival village with food kiosks and live music on weekends, and many multiethnic food choices in the downtown and surrounding

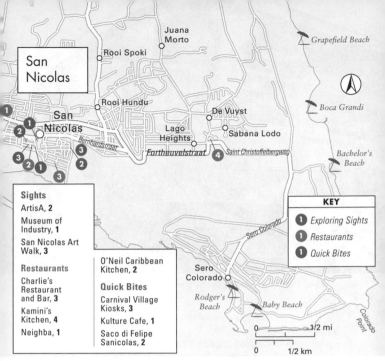

San Nicolas

Sights
ArtisA, **2**
Museum of Industry, **1**
San Nicolas Art Walk, **3**

Restaurants
Charlie's Restaurant and Bar, **3**
Kamini's Kitchen, **4**
Neighba, **1**

O'Neil Caribbean Kitchen, **2**

Quick Bites
Carnival Village Kiosks, **3**
Kulture Cafe, **1**
Saco di Felipe Sanicolas, **2**

KEY
1 Exploring Sights
1 Restaurants
1 Quick Bites

regions. Pop-up street festivals and farmers' markets continue to introduce visitors to the unique charms of Sunrise City, and the legendary Charlie's Bar and Restaurant, a family-run business that's been around since 1941, continues to draw patrons from around the world.

Development in the seafront area around Seroe Colorado has begun for a new all-inclusive resort, and the Baby Beach area is also being expanded and improved to accommodate more tourism.

Sights

★ ArtisA

ARTS CENTER | Housed in a gorgeous glassed-in affair right downtown, ArtisA (Art is Aruba) is part art gallery and part of the administrative foundation that is largely responsible for the art and culture revolution in San Nicolas. Rotating exhibits showcase local artists, and visitors can purchase works on site or from their large online collection. This is also where you can purchase tickets to the guided art walk tours (also available online.) The ethereal space hosts workshops; the foundation has also begun hosting special events like "art-meets-cuisine," where local chefs offer a

The beautiful murals found on San Nicolas's Art Walk began in 2015.

dining experience inspired by the local artists, sometimes with local musicians on site, too. They plan to open a second "fun" gallery nearby called Space21.art that will serve cocktails and tapas and act as a cultural socializing hub. ✉ *Bernard van de Veen Zeppenfeldstraat 6, San Nicolaas* ☎ *297/593–4475* ⊕ *artisaruba. com* ☾ *Closed Sun.*

★ Museum of Industry
The old water tower in San Nicolas has been beautifully restored into a modern interactive museum chronicling the different types of industries that have fueled the island's economy over the past two centuries. Phosphate, gold, oil, and aloe all played major parts in the island's fortunes until tourism became Aruba's main economic driver. Displays include artifacts and profiles of colorful characters who played big roles in different eras. One of the highlights is the culture wall, a mural consisting of portraits of locals through the ages, all leading up the glassed-in walls of the old tower staircase. ✉ *Water Tower, Bernhardstraat 164, San Nicolaas* ☎ *297/584–7090* ⊕ *www.facebook.com/moiaruba* ✉ *$5* ☾ *Closed weekends.*

San Nicolas Art Walk
PUBLIC ART | In the past few years, San Nicolas has seen an extraordinary revitalization and beautification thanks to new art initiatives organized by the local artists' foundation, ArtisA (Art is Aruba). What began as a simple mural project in 2015 has since blossomed into the establishment of an annual Aruba Art Fair, whose aim is to create more public art projects every year. Today,

incredible murals cover entire buildings, and there are sculptures and mosaic benches scattered around town. Self-guided tours are possible, but a guided tour provides insight into the artists, the inspiration behind their work, and access to all the visual effects included in the new interactive art. ⊠ *San Nicolaas* ⊕ *arubamural-tours.com.*

 Beaches

The beaches surrounding San Nicolas range from pristine soft sand edged by aqua waters to wild and windswept windsurfing and kiteboarding hot spots where the pros practice (not for amateurs.) There are also romantic yet unswimmable picturesque escapes ideal for picnics in solitude.

★ Baby Beach

BEACH | FAMILY | On the island's Eastern Tip (near the refinery), this semicircular beach borders a placid bay of turquoise water that's about as shallow as a wading pool—perfect for families with little ones. A small coral reef basin at the sea's edge offers superb snorkeling, but do not pass the barrier—the current is extremely strong outside the rocks. JADS Dive Center offers snorkel equipment rentals, and this is a popular place to see and swim with sea turtles, too. Rum Reef on one end is a unique adults-only bar and infinity pool overlooking the beach, and below it is a family-friendly beach and snack bar. On the other end you can rent clamshell shade tents and lounges on the beach from Big Mama Grill, also a family-friendly gathering spot. **Amenities:** food and drink; showers; toilets; parking (free); **Best for:** snorkeling; swimming. ⊠ *Seroe Colorado.*

Bachelor's Beach

BEACH | This eastside beach is known for its white-powder sand. Snorkeling can be good, but bring a guide. The conditions aren't the best for swimming, as the currents can be strong. **Amenities:** none. **Best for:** snorkeling; windsurfing. ⊠ *East end, south of Boca Grandi* ⊹ *East end, south of Boca Grandi.*

Boca Grandi

BEACH | This is *the* choice for the island's best kiteboarders and expert windsurfers—even more so than Fisherman's Huts—but the currents are seriously strong, so it's not safe for casual swimming. It's very picturesque, though, and a perfect spot for a picnic. It's a few minutes from San Nicolas proper; look for the big red anchor or the kites in the air. Be forewarned: the conditions are not for amateurs, and there are no lifeguards or facilities nearby, should you get into trouble. **Amenities:** parking (free). **Best for:**

Baby Beach is a great spot for families.

solitude; walking; windsurfing. ⊠ *San Nicolaas* ✢ *East end, near Seagrape Grove.*

Grapefield Beach

BEACH | Just north of Boca Grandi on the eastern coast, a sweep of blinding-white sand in the shadow of cliffs and boulders is marked by an anchor-shape memorial dedicated to seamen. Pick sea grapes from January to June. Swimming is not recommended, as the waves here can be rough. This is not a popular tourist beach, so finding a quiet spot is almost guaranteed, but the downside of this is a complete lack of facilities or nearby refreshments. **Amenities:** none. **Best for:** solitude. ✢ *East end, southwest of San Nicolas.*

★ Rodger's Beach

BEACH | Near Baby Beach on the island's Eastern Tip, this beautiful curving stretch of sand is only slightly marred by its proximity to the tanks and towers of the oil refinery at the bay's far side. Look for the gorgeous, recently decorated mosaic stairs descending to the sand; the swimming conditions are excellent here. It's usually very quiet during the week, so you might have the beach all to yourself, but it's a local favorite on weekends. Full facilities can be found next door at JADS Dive Center strip on Baby Beach. **Amenities:** food and drink; toilets; parking (free). **Best for:** swimming; solitude. ⊠ *Seroe Colorado* ✢ *Next to Baby Beach.*

6

🍴 Restaurants

During Aruba's oil boom, San Nicolas became a cultural melting pot as many workers brought their own flavors of food to the island. Today, you'll find everything from Jamaican and Trinidadian cuisines to South American and Asian, usually all with an Aruban twist. There is modern urban fare, too, like barista-style coffees, wraps, and great breakfasts at the Kulture Cafe at the historic Nicolaas Store. For really local fare be sure to seek out the *sacos*, a San Nicolas specialty that consists of a brown paper bag filled with finger-licking-good items like ribs, chicken, pork chops, johnnycakes, fried potatoes, corn on the cob, or plantains. Sacos are so well-known that locals and repeat visitors in the know often make a special trip from the other end of the island for them, usually with a stop at Saco di Felipe, a hole-in-the-wall spot that's been in business for six decades. Yes, it's greasy, but that's the point, and it's addictive. Just don't ask for cutlery, as you're supposed to eat it all with your hands.

★ Charlie's Restaurant and Bar

$$$ | CARIBBEAN | Since 1941, Charlie's has been the heart and soul of San Nicolas, famous for its interior decorated with eclectic bric-a-brac left behind by decades of international visitors. It also serves surprisingly good food, including delicious fresh fish and shrimp and killer steaks. **Known for:** a legendary San Nicolas institution; Boozer Coladas, the signature drink; third-generation owner named Charles. ⑤ *Average main: $25* ⊠ *Bernard van de Veen Zeppenfeldstraat 56, San Nicolaas* ☎ *297/584–5086* ⊕ *www. charliesbararuba.com* ⊘ *Closed Sun.*

★ Kamini's Kitchen

$$ | CARIBBEAN | Housed in a cheery blue-and-green cottage, this charming spot is run by Kamini Kurvink, who combines her Trinidadian heritage with local flavors to create unique Caribbean comfort food. Fish, seafood, and meat dishes are served with a spicy flair thanks to Kamini's secret signature hot sauces. **Known for:** hearty portions of homemade Caribbean specialties, like goat curry and chicken roti; a great selection of vegetarian options; very warm, welcoming, and friendly staff and owner. ⑤ *Average main: $12* ⊠ *De Vuyst 41B, San Nicolaas* ☎ *297/587–1398* ⊕ *www. facebook.com/KaminisKitchen* ⊘ *Closed Tues.*

O'Niel Caribbean Kitchen

$$ | CARIBBEAN | FAMILY | Right smack in the middle of the San Nicolas Art Walk, O'Niel's is a warm and welcoming eatery that's an ideal spot to get your Jamaican jerk on. Real-deal Jamaican dishes like ackee with saltfish and oxtail with beans are menu

favorites, but there are also local Aruban specialties like goat stew and fresh local seafood; vegetarian and vegan dishes are also available. **Known for:** coconut-infused dishes like shrimp or chicken with rum and sweet chili sauce; real-deal Jamaican specialties like ackee with saltfish; local favorite gathering spot. $ *Average main: $15* ✉ *Bernard van de Veen Zeppenfeldstraat 15, San Nicolaas* ☎ *297/584–8700* ⊕ *www.facebook.com/OnielCaribbeanKitchen297* ☽ *Closed Mon.*

★ Neighba

$$ | **CARIBBEAN** | Rising like a phoenix from a vacant lot, this funky new gathering place specializes in creative modern cuisine and handcrafted cocktails in an alfresco bar/garden setting with eye-popping outdoor art. The eclectic menu, though small, includes authentic Aruban flavors like *sanger yena* (blood sausage) and Dutch fusion dishes like Gouda spring rolls and popcorn chicken waffles with peanut sauce. **Known for:** creative contemporary Caribbean and international fusion cuisine; Sunday BBQs with live music; special events like soca bingo night or wine and jazz get-togethers. $ *Average main: $18* ✉ *Bernhardstraat 75C, San Nicolaas* ☎ *297/745–5850 WhatsApp, 297/586–5588* ⊕ *www. facebook.com/Neighba.aruba* ☽ *Closed Tues.*

☕ Coffee and Quick Bites

Carnival Village Kiosks

$ | **CARIBBEAN** | Colorful wooden kiosks fill the area around the outside of the fenced-in square with folks offering food truck–style fare and cold drinks. They are not all open every day, but there is usually one open at any given time (and only after 11 am). **Known for:** authentic local fare like johnnycakes and saltfish; great prices for big portions; most kiosks are licensed to serve beer. $ *Average main: $8* ✉ *Lagoweg, San Nicolaas* 🖃 *No credit cards.*

★ Kulture Cafe

$ | **CAFÉ** | The café in the beautifully restored historic Nicolaas Store in the heart of downtown San Nicolas serves up great barista-style hot and iced coffees and snacks. With seating indoors or out, this is an ideal pit stop before or after exploring the outdoor art. **Known for:** excellent wraps and panini; great local and American-style breakfasts; ice cream and decadent desserts like caramel–sea salt cheesecake. $ *Average main: $7* ✉ *Bernard van de Veen Zeppenfeldstraat 27, San Nicolaas* ☎ *297/280–5566* ⊕ *www.facebook. com/Kulturecafearuba.*

Saco di Felipe Sanicolas

,$ | **CARIBBEAN** | This hole-in-the-wall is *the* place for the best sacos, paper bags full of fried chicken, ribs, chops, plantains, fries, and johnnycakes. It's the perfect snack before—or after—a night out. **Known for:** local flavor; sacos are known as a "heart attack in a bag" but they're so worth it; all fried fare makes an especially hearty snack for after barhopping. $ *Average main: $10* ⌂ *St. Maarten Straat, San Nicolaas* ☎ *297/584–5723* ⊕ *www.facebook. com/saco.felipe* ▤ *No credit cards* ☉ *No lunch.*

Hotels

Places to stay are few and far between in San Nicolas proper, but that might change in the next few years, as there are big plans for an area that once housed Americans working at the oil refinery in Seroe Colorado in the '40s and '50s. With that said, if you really want to be in the area, you might find an Airbnb close to Baby Beach or Rodger's Beach. The closest boutique hotels are in Savaneta.

ⓨ Nightlife

Unless there's a street festival going on, San Nicolas's nightlife is confined to a few local spots that occasionally have live music outside—like the new Carnival Village—but the town is not really a place for barhopping. Most of the little bars double as brothels that are part of the small but legal red-light district. However, when there is a scheduled street festival or annual event, like Aruba Art Week, it's very safe for everyone (including families) after dark, and the events are well worth attending.

ⓐ Performing Arts

Principal Cinema

FILM | **FAMILY** | After nearly three decades, locals are delighted to have a modern cinema in San Nicolas again. The air-conditioned theater is state-of-the-art with large screens, VIP seats, and a modern concession stand. It's an ideal place to catch a flick before or after an afternoon at Baby Beach or the art walk. ⌂ *Stuyvesantstraat 20, San Nicolaas* ✛ *In the main promenade downtown* ☎ *297/523–6844* ⊕ *www.themoviesaruba.com/sannicolas* ☉ *Closed Mon.–Wed.*

Shopping

There are lots of mom-and-pop shops, clothing stores, small department stores, mini-markets and grocery outlets, modern pharmacies, and a few hardware stores scattered about, so you'll have no problem finding anything you forgot to bring out on a day trip. If you're seeking high-end unique souvenirs, then ArtisA Gallery has lovely locally made art pieces.

Savaneta

It might be hard to believe that this sleepy little community on the southeastern coast was once Aruba's first capital city, but it was, until 1797. The Dutch commanders made their residences here, and this is where the island's first stone house was built as the governor's residence. Today, this popular fishing spot is very much a local neighborhood with an easy laid-back vibe and some new boho-chic places to stay and eat. There are pop-up farmers' markets, arts and crafts fairs, and social get-togethers, as well as a new foundation dedicated to putting this lovely little area back on the map, launched with the motto "I Love Savaneta." This little town is also home to the island's only Olympic-size public swimming pool. That's where they train their Olympic contenders—the island sent swimmers to the Summer Olympics in 2016 and 2021. It's also home to the Royal Netherlands Navy, the Netherlands Marine Corps, and the Netherlands Coast Guard, so don't be surprised to see their ships gliding by often and close to shore. Don't be shy to wave—they like that.

🏖 Beaches

Savaneta is not really a beach community, as most of the swimming is done by jumping off a dock or deck, so don't except to see long strands of soft white sand like other parts of the island. Mangel Halto and the little stretch at Santo Largo are the exceptions.

Mangel Halto (*Savaneta Beach*)
BEACH | Though technically in the region called Pos Chiquito, this beach is at the very beginning of Savaneta. With a purposely scuttled boat wreck near the coast and a lot to see outside the bay, this is one of the most popular spots for shore diving, but be aware that currents are strong once you're outside the cove. It's also popular for picnics, and a wooden dock and stairs into the ocean make getting into the water easy. Sea kayak tours depart from here, and some outfits offer power snorkeling and regular

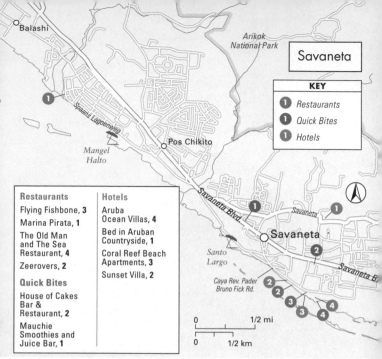

Savaneta

KEY	
1	Restaurants
1	Quick Bites
1	Hotels

Restaurants

Flying Fishbone, **3**

Marina Pirata, **1**

The Old Man and The Sea Restaurant, **4**

Zeerovers, **2**

Quick Bites

House of Cakes Bar & Restaurant, **2**

Mauchie Smoothies and Juice Bar, **1**

Hotels

Aruba Ocean Villas, **4**

Bed in Aruban Countryside, **1**

Coral Reef Beach Apartments, **3**

Sunset Villa, **2**

snorkeling as well. There are stores within easy walking distance for food and drink. There are very few *palapas*, but you can take shade under the many trees and mangroves. **Amenities:** water sports. **Best for:** snorkeling; swimming. ⊠ *Savaneta* ✛ *Between Savaneta proper and Pos Chiquito.*

Santo Largo

BEACH | This small pristine beach in between Mangel Halto and Governor's Bay (just before Flying Fishbone) makes an ideal picnic spot far away from the crowds. Swimming conditions are good—thanks to shallow water edged by white-powder sand—but there are no facilities and virtually no shade. **Amenities:** none. **Best for:** swimming. ⊠ *San Nicolaas.*

🍽 Restaurants

Little cafés, snack bars, and Asian food take-out spots can be found around town, but for the best eats and fine dining head to the few waterfront spots peppered along the coastline.

★ Flying Fishbone

$$$$ | INTERNATIONAL | Opened in 1977, this was the first restaurant in Aruba to offer feet-in-the-water dining, and its insanely romantic seaside setting is why this legendary landmark is so worth the trek out to Savaneta. An international menu is designed to please all palates, but the real culinary draw is fish straight from the island's most famous local fisherman's pier, located a few doors over. **Known for:** "Savaneta's Seafood History" featuring the very local catch of the day; individual-size baked Alaska, flambéed table-side; tables set right in the ocean. $ *Average main: $40* ✉ *Savaneta 344, Savaneta* ☎ *297/584–2506* ⊕ *www.flyingfish-bone.com* ☾ *No lunch.*

Marina Pirata

$$$ | CARIBBEAN | FAMILY | Locals and regular visitors in the know flock to this off-the-radar boathouse-style restaurant for fresh fish and seafood, as well as the melt-in-your-mouth filet. Spectacular sunset views are a given, and kids love seeing the abundant fish swimming all around the illuminated pier at night with underwater lights. **Known for:** fresh local lobster served different ways; great place for group celebrations; many squid dishes. $ *Average main: $25* ✉ *Spanish Waters, Spaans Lagoenweg 4, Savaneta* ☎ *297/585–7150* ⊕ *www.facebook.com/Marinapirataaruba* ☾ *Closed Tues. No lunch.*

★ The Old Man and The Sea Restaurant

$$$$ | CARIBBEAN | The signature restaurant of Aruba Ocean Villas is tiny, but it's well worth the trip for the romantic, toes-in-the-sand, adults-only dining experience with soft music and twinkling lights. The eclectic menu revolves around local seafood and fine quality meats with authentic Aruban specialties like *keshi yena* (stuffed cheese casserole). **Known for:** fresh catch of the day; perfectly prepared surf-and-turf; one of the few places to get New Zealand rack of lamb. $ *Average main: $55* ✉ *Savaneta 356A, Savaneta* ☎ *297/584–3434* ⊕ *www.arubaoceanvillas.com/restaurant* ☾ *No lunch.*

Zeerovers

$ | CARIBBEAN | FAMILY | With a name that means "pirates" in Dutch, this alfresco restaurant sits right on the Savaneta pier, where the local fishermen bring in their daily catch. The menu is basic: the day's fish and other seafood, fried almost as soon as it's lifted out of the boat and served with sides of local staples like fried plantains. **Known for:** freshest fish on the island; lively local hangout; picturesque sea view and sunsets. $ *Average main: $10* ✉ *Savaneta Pier, Savaneta 270A, Savaneta* ☎ *297/584–8401* ⊕ *www.facebook.com/zeerovers* ☾ *Closed Mon. and Tues.*

Located just before Savaneta, Mangel Halto is a popular spot for shore diving, kayaking, and picnics.

☕ Coffee and Quick Bites

House of Cakes Bar & Restaurant

$ | **INTERNATIONAL** | About 10 minutes past the airport en route to San Nicolas, this cheery little spot serves a lot more than baked goods and authentic Aruban cakes by the slice. They are also popular for their breakfasts, occasional weekend BBQs, and great snack platters to go. **Known for:** fresh cakes, pastries, and sweets; all-you-can-eat weekend breakfast; local fare lunch specials. ⑤ *Average main: $10* ⊠ *Rte. 1, Savaneta* ☎ *297/584–2323* ⊕ *houseofcakes.business.site.*

Mauchie Smoothies and Juice Bar

$ | **INTERNATIONAL** | This colorful roadside stand, just before the Savaneta turn, has excellent smoothies and fresh juices, as well as healthy wraps and acai bowls. They also sell great organic herbal remedies made from local produce and have recently opened a second outlet in San Nicolas. **Known for:** organic and locally sourced juices; great smoothies made with local produce; healthy snacks to go. ⑤ *Average main: $8* ⊠ *New Winter Garden, Savaneta 87, Savaneta* ☎ *297/584–7115* ⊕ *www.facebook.com/mauchismoothies.*

Hotels

Most of the accommodations in the Savaneta area are private home rentals or rooms available via Airbnb, but one notable exception is the luxurious South Pacific–style oasis called Aruba Ocean Villas.

★ Aruba Ocean Villas
$$$$ | RESORT | This stunning adults-only luxury boutique resort brings romance South Pacific–style to Savaneta with Aruba's only overwater bungalows—some two-story penthouse extravaganzas, some inviting Bali bamboo-style beach houses and villas, and one unique two-story treehouse. **Pros:** insanely romantic setting, ideal for honeymoons; luxurious elite vibe yet friendly staff; far from the tourist fray. **Cons:** a car is needed; no pool in common area; little entertainment. ⑤ *Rooms from: $600* ⊠ *Savaneta 356A, Savaneta* ⊕ *A few doors down from the Flying Fishbone* ☎ *297/584–3434, 877/920–1381 in the U.S.* ⊕ *www.arubaoceanvillas.com* ⇴ *13 villas* ❏ *Free Breakfast.*

Bed in Aruban Countryside
$ | APARTMENT | In this charming complex, brightly colored cottage-style studios have their own kitchens, and guests have access to a garden patio and gazebos, a modern barbecue, and a large communal table—plus it's only a 5-minute drive to Mangel Halto Beach. **Pros:** a great stay for animal lovers; authentic local experience; budget-friendly, clean, and well kept. **Cons:** not on a beach; you need a car to get around; no dining on-site. ⑤ *Rooms from: $70* ⊠ *Seroe Alejandro 6, Savaneta* ☎ *297/593–2933* ⇴ *4 studio apartments* ❏ *No Meals* ⌥ *1 night minimum. Discounted prices for long-term rentals.*

Coral Reef Beach Apartments
$ | HOTEL | This beachfront complex with apartment-style rooms has a fully stocked communal kitchen for guests to self-cater and a tiny private beach and deck with an abundance of hammocks and picnic tables. **Pros:** bright fresh rooms, some with great sea views; two large suites are great for families on a budget; maid service and Wi-Fi included. **Cons:** rooms do not have hot water; communal kitchen is not always convenient for everyone; not all rooms have sea views. ⑤ *Rooms from: $210* ⊠ *Savaneta 344A, Savaneta* ☎ *297/584–7764* ⊕ *www.coralreefbeachapartments.com* ⇴ *8 units* ❏ *No Meals* ⌥ *3-night minimum.*

★ Sunset Villa

$$$$ | **HOUSE** | **FAMILY** | Once home to the owner of Aruba Ocean Villas and only bookable through their website, this incredible semi-overwater complex a few doors down from the main resort holds all kinds of surprises. **Pros:** spacious retreat full of unique decor and luxury amenities; yoga mats, snorkels, floaties, etc. all included; housekeeping available. **Cons:** no laundry facilities; families with toddlers should be vigilant on the deck, as it has no rails; far from shopping, so you'll need a car. ⑤ *Rooms from: $1299* ⊠ *Savaneta 258B, Savaneta* ☎ *297/584–3434* ⊕ *www.arubaocean-villas.com/sunset-villa* ⌁ *1 unit* ⎮⊙⎮ *No Meals.*

🛍 Shopping

There's not much shopping per se around Savaneta, save a handful of mini-markets and general supply stores. Occasional pop-up festivals with local farmers and craftspeople occur but are not regularly scheduled.

ARIKOK NATIONAL PARK AND ENVIRONS

Updated by
Susan Campbell

👁 Sights   🍴 Restaurants   🛏 Hotels   🛍 Shopping   🍸 Nightlife

★★★★★   ★☆☆☆☆   ☆☆☆☆☆   ☆☆☆☆☆   ☆☆☆☆☆

NEIGHBORHOOD SNAPSHOT

TOP EXPERIENCES

■ **Go Wild:** Discover the park's untamed wilderness with a guided tour on foot or by vehicle.

■ **Cool off in Caves and Conchi:** Swim in the surreal natural pool or explore ancient caves.

■ **Hike the Haystack:** Climb Mt. Hooiberg—the island's second-highest peak—for bragging rights and a great view.

■ **Climb Casibari:** Discover odd rock formations that look like something out of The Flintstones.

■ **Go for the Gold:** Trek around the ruins of Aruba's main gold smelter by the sea at Bushiribana.

GETTING HERE AND AROUND

A few main highways lead to the national park entrance. Depending on where you are coming from—Palm Beach, Eagle Beach, or Oranjestad—it's best to check a map for the fastest route. It's also best to take a guided tour of the park to get your bearings, as it can be an unforgiving outback in many places and definitely requires a four-wheel-drive vehicle. If you're coming from San Nicolas, there's a separate entrance with a small admission kiosk, but no visitor center.

PLANNING YOUR TIME

The interior region is best explored during daylight hours, as there's little to do at night and not well lit. The park closes at 4 pm; overnight camping is not allowed. If you plan on hiking in the park, go early, because it gets very hot in the afternoon and there's little shade.

VIEWFINDER

■ One of the most popular spots for stunning shots in Arikok National Park has always been the natural pool, known as *Conchi*, but the photo-ops at Dos Playa are pretty spectacular, too. Snap a selfie there with the dramatic contours and contrasts of crashing aqua waves, white sand coves, and craggy cliffs as your backdrop. Though the interiors of the caves are also Insta-worthy, no flash photography is permitted. Also note that drone photography isn't permitted within the park so as not to disturb nature. The ruins of the gold mines also provide Insta-worthy shots, as you can climb them and frame yourself in a window frame with the sea as your background.

First-time visitors are often surprised to discover how desert like the other side of Aruba becomes once you explore away from the landscaped grounds of the resorts, with their swaying palms and brightly colored blooms. The island's interior and northeast coast are arid, rocky, and wild, but they have their own unique beauty and are well worth exploring for surreal scenic vistas, romantic wave-whipped cliffs, and vast expanses of untouched wilderness.

Arikok National Park takes up approximately 20% of the island and is fiercely protected due to its fragile ecosystem; visitors must pay a park fee and abide by park rules in order to enjoy it. Off-roading is no longer allowed. Within the park there are many surprises beyond cacti forests, dry riverbeds, and twisted divi-divi trees. There are cool caves like Fontein and Quadirikiri, a remote natural pool known as Conchi, and Mt. Jamanota, the island's highest peak. Meandering goats and donkeys are common, but the park's elusive wildlife is easier to discover with the help of a guide. Park rangers offer free tours and man the entrances to the caves to enlighten visitors about their ancient history.

Surrounding the park in the interior are neighborhoods worth exploring if you want to see how the locals live, like Santa Cruz, where you should sleuth out the numerous "snacks"—small food outlets that serve great homemade fare at very low prices. ■TIP→ **Make sure you have cash, as many places don't take credit cards.**

There's also Paradera, a small interior neighborhood where you'll find three natural attractions—the Casibari and Ayo rock formations and Mt. Hooiberg ("The Haystack")—all worth a visit on their own.

Exploring Arikok National Park

Visitors are free to hike on their own through Arikok National Park, and hiking maps are free at the Arikok Visitor Center. However, there's so much to see in the park in terms of flora and fauna, and so many fascinating facts about the island's fragile ecosystem and indigenous creatures, that a guide is invaluable. Luckily, free mini guided tours with a park ranger are available at the visitor center—reservations must be made 48 hours in advance—and are well worth it, especially for first-time visitors.

DID YOU KNOW?
Aruba is home to one of the world's rarest rattlesnakes. There are only about 200 Cascabel rattlesnakes in existence, and they are only found naturally on this island. The park is home to the majority, but they are elusive and shy and rarely stay out in the hot sun past 11 am. However, if you do hear a loud rattlesnake noise when you're passing a hole in the ground, don't freak out. Chances are good that it's an Aruban burrowing owl—or "shoco," as it's known on the island. This quirky burrowing owl mimics the sound of a rattlesnake to keep predators away from its underground home.

The little red berries found on top of the Turk's Cap cactus are edible—and delicious. Just be careful if you try to pick them, as these cacti are very prickly. The cacti are an important food source for the island's bird population.

Arikok National Park

Aruba's national park encompasses 7,907 acres. Guests can explore the island's untamed wilderness by regular car or 4x4 vehicle, horseback, or guided tour with a park ranger or tour operator. Personally driven ATVs, UTVs, motorcycles, and the like are no longer allowed in the park; only guided tours with these vehicles are permitted. The park's natural wonders include cool caves, a remote natural pool to swim and snorkel in, as well as the island's tallest peak, Mt. Jamanota, which is only recommended for experienced hikers. It also extends now to the Spanish Lagoon region to protect the area's waterways and mangroves.

◉ Sights

★ Arikok National Park

NATIONAL PARK | Covering almost 20% of the island's landmass, this protected preserve of arid cacti-studded outback has interesting nature and wildlife if you know where to look. There are close to 30 miles of hiking trails within the park zone, including a trek up Mt. Jamanota, the island's highest peak. Hiking maps for all levels of hikers are free at the visitor center, and in-depth maps of the park and its attractions are also available for download online at their website. It's highly recommended to take a guided tour on foot or by vehicle, as the roads can be very rough in some places; there are plenty of excursions by ATV, UTV, Jeep safaris, and more. A guided preview of what you can expect will help you if you want to return in your own rental car as well, but keep in mind that a 4x4 vehicle is a must and all visitors must pay a park entrance fee, which helps fund the park's conservation. Some trails lead to glorious seaside coastal views, but a guided tour will help you understand the significance of the region and help you find attractions like the caves on the northeastern coast. There are no facilities past the visitor center so bring plenty of water and sunscreen and wear good shoes, as the terrain is very rocky. A new region near Spanish Lagoon has also been added recently as part of its protected area due to the importance of its freshwater canals and mangrove forests, but it is closer to Savaneta on the southwest coast and not within the original park confines. There is also an entrance to the park closer to San Nicolas at the Van Piet wind farm; there is a small kiosk there to pay your entrance fee and get information, but no facilities. ■TIP→ **You can book free guided hikes with a park ranger by phone or email, but you must reserve 48 hours in advance.** ⊠ *San Fuego 70, Arikok National Park* ☎ *297/585–1234* ⊕ *www.arubanationalpark.org* ⊠ *$15* ⌁ *Park closes daily at 4 pm.*

Arikok Visitor Center

VISITOR CENTER | **FAMILY** | At the park's main entrance, Arikok Visitor Center houses offices, restrooms, and food facilities. All visitors must stop here upon entering so that officials can manage the traffic flow and hand out information on park rules and features. ■TIP→ **If you intend to spend a lot of your holiday hiking in or simply exploring the park, consider purchasing a yearly pass for $50 (a day pass is $15).** ⊠ *San Fuego 70, Arikok National Park* ☎ *297/585–1234* ⊕ *www.arubanationalpark.org/main/visitor-center/.*

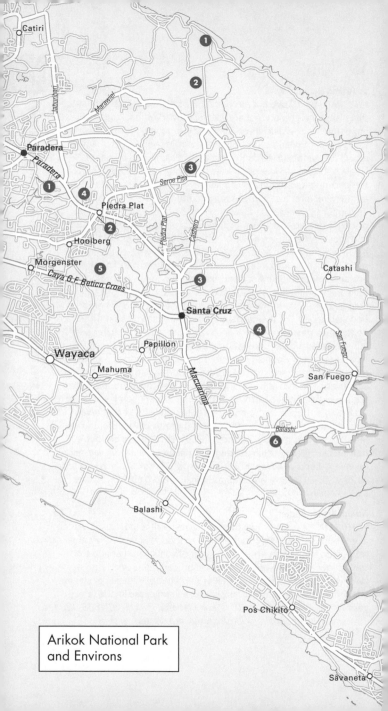

Arikok National Park
and Environs

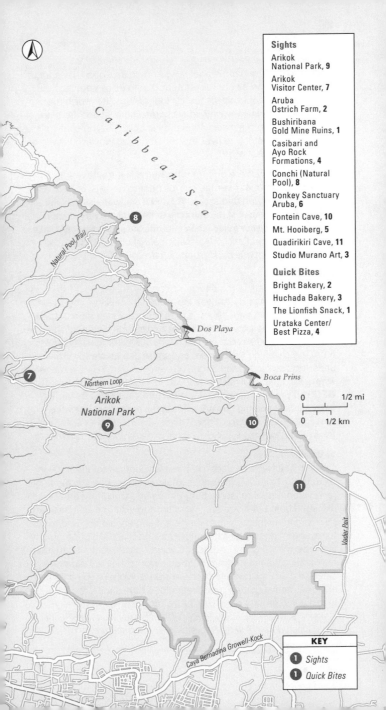

Caribbean Sea

Sights

Arikok
National Park, **9**

Arikok
Visitor Center, **7**

Aruba
Ostrich Farm, **2**

Bushiribana
Gold Mine Ruins, **1**

Casibari and
Ayo Rock
Formations, **4**

Conchi (Natural
Pool), **8**

Donkey Sanctuary
Aruba, **6**

Fontein Cave, **10**

Mt. Hooiberg, **5**

Quadirikiri Cave, **11**

Studio Murano Art, **3**

Quick Bites

Bright Bakery, **2**

Huchada Bakery, **3**

The Lionfish Snack, **1**

Urataka Center/
Best Pizza, **4**

Natural Pool Trail

Dos Playa

Boca Prins

Northern Loop

*Arikok
National Park*

Vader Piet

Caya Bernadina Growell-Kock

0   1/2 mi
0   1/2 km

KEY
1 *Sights*
1 *Quick Bites*

★ Conchi (Natural Pool)

NATURE SIGHT | The natural pool, also known as *Conchi*, meaning "bowl," was once a very secret spot due to its remote location, but today it's frequently visited by tour groups. It's worth the trip though—the scene of wild surf crashing over ancient black volcanic rocks into a placid aqua pool is epic, and the spray of the cold seawater shooting over the top upon you while you swim or snorkel is exhilarating.

You can also hike here on foot with Aruba Nature Adventures or drive your own 4x4 rental, but it's best to go with guides, as the roads are rough and steep. ■TIP→ **Bring water shoes with a good grip; the rocks at the entrance to the pool are very slippery. Listen closely to your guide when entering the pool for safety's sake.** ⊠ *Arikok National Park, Arikok National Park* ☎ *297/585–1234* ⊕ *www.arubanationalpark.org/main/attractions/.*

Fontein Cave

CAVE | **FAMILY** | This is the park's most popular cave as it's the only one with drawings by Arawak Indians on its ceilings. The caves are accessible during park hours, and rangers are stationed outside the cave and can provide tours that explain the history of the cave drawings as well as discuss the resident stalagmites and stalactites. The cave floor is uneven, and there can be creepy crawlies underfoot, so closed-toe shoes are encouraged. Ask the ranger where the little pool is nearby if you want a free fish pedicure! ■TIP→ **If you have time, check out the two-chambered Quadirikiri Cave; sunlight pouring through holes in the cave's roof lights the space.** ⊠ *Arikok National Park, Arikok National Park* ⊹ *Off Rte 7 (Northern Loop)* ☎ *297/585–1234* ⊕ *www.arubanationalpark.org.*

★ Quadirikiri Cave

CAVE | Arikok National Park has three ancient caves under its protection, Huliba (aka Tunnel of Love) is no longer open to the public for environmental reasons, but Fontein and Quadirikiri are. Quadiriki is the best bet if you only have time to visit one as it has natural skylights within which are ethereal and enchanting and make for excellent photographs. Be forewarned that flash photography is not permitted as it disturbs the hundreds of resident bats that make this cave their home, but don't worry, they are harmless and sleep all day. Park rangers at the entrance will take you on a free and informative guided tour. Wear closed-toe shoes, the interior is rocky and ground bugs live there, too. ⊠ *Arikok National Park, Arikok National Park* ☎ *297/585–1234* ⊕ *www.arubanationalpark. org* ⊠ *included in Arikok National Park entrance fee.*

The natural pool, or Conchi, was once a secret spot due to its remote location.

 Beaches

Boca Prins

BEACH | You'll need a four-wheel-drive vehicle to make the trek to this strip of coastline near Fontein Cave and Blue Lagoon. Famous for its backdrop of stunning sand dunes, the beach itself is small, but with two rocky cliffs and crashing waves, it's as romantic as Aruba gets. The water is rough and swimming is prohibited, but it's a perfect picnic stop. Wear sturdy shoes, as the beach is rocky. **Amenities:** none. **Best for:** walking; solitude. ✛ *Off Rte. 7A/B, near Fontein Cave.*

Dos Playa

BEACH | One of the most photogenic picnic spots on the island, this beach is two coves divided by limestone cliffs. One is treasured by surfers for its rolling waves; the other looks placid but has a current that is far too strong for swimming—you'll have to settle for sunbathing only. The best access is by four-wheel drive, as it's within the boundaries of rugged Arikok National Park, but do not drive on the sand or rocks. You might see locals surfing, but unless you are a pro, don't try it yourself—the current is dangerously strong. **Amenities:** none. **Best for:** walking; solitude. ✛ *Just north of Boca Prins.*

Arikok National Park's Dos Playa is a great spot for photos, picnics, and solitude.

🍽 Restaurants

Though you can get some cold drinks and small snacks at the Arikok Park Visitor Center, you should bring your own water, as there are no food or drink outlets in the park. And please don't leave behind any litter if you bring your own food and drink.

Arikok National Park Environs: Santa Cruz and Paradera

The area surrounding Arikok National Park, including the towns of Santa Cruz and Paradera, offers offbeat attractions with unexpected animals and the island's second-highest peak, Mt. Hooiberg. There are also romantic secluded spots for picnics and unique scenic vistas for photo ops.

Make time to explore the local neighborhoods to see the cunucu houses where many of the local residents live, and stop in Ayo to visit a great outdoor restaurant and glassblowing studio. There are other places to grab lunch and snacks, but there aren't places to stay, shop, or go out at night, so plan to visit the area as a day trip.

Cunucu Houses

Pastel houses surrounded by cacti fences adorn Aruba's flat rugged *cunucu* ("country" in Papiamento). The features of these traditional houses were developed in response to the environment. Early settlers discovered that slanting roofs allowed the heat to rise and that small windows helped keep in the cool air. Among the earliest building materials was *caliche*, a durable calcium-carbonate substance found in the island's southeastern hills. Many houses were also built using interlocking coral rocks that didn't require mortar (this technique is no longer used, thanks to cement and concrete). Contemporary design combines some of the basic principles of the earlier homes with touches of modernization: windows, though still narrow, have been elongated; roofs are constructed of bright tiles; pretty patios have been added; and doorways and balconies present an ornamental face to the world beyond. Though modernized today, you might still see fences made of cacti to keep the pesky wild goats out of people's precious gardens.

◉ Sights

Aruba Ostrich Farm

FARM/RANCH | FAMILY | Everything you ever wanted to know about the world's largest living birds can be found at this farm and ranch. There are emus, too. A large *palapa* (palm-thatched roof) houses a gift shop and restaurant that draws large bus tours, and tours of the farm are available every half hour starting at 10 am until 3 pm, seven days a week. Feeding the ostriches is fun, and you can also hold an egg in your hands. There is a full-service restaurant on-site as well as a farmers' market (check Facebook for dates), and the souvenir shop sells unique locally made crafts and keepsakes. ✉ *Matividiri 57, Paradera* ☎ *297/585–9630* ⊕ *www.arubaostrich-farm.com* 🎟 *$14.*

Bushiribana Gold Mine Ruins

HISTORIC SIGHT | You can view what is left of Aruba's one-time gold rush at the seaside ruins of a gold smelter; it's a great spot for photo ops and you are welcome to climb throughout the old rock structure. The restless north coast waters there are picturesque, with lots of crashing spray on the cliffs. It's ironic that the Spanish left the island alone basically because they thought it was worthless; in fact, they dubbed it *isla inutil* (useless island) since they thought it had no gold or silver, but locals did find some long after the Spanish left. There's always a great snack truck parked there (Bushiribana Happy Stop) with a surprisingly eclectic selection of hearty fare. ∎TIP➜ **Go early in the morning, before the multitude of tours arrive, if you want the ruins to yourself for the best photos.** ⊠ *North Coast, Bushiribana* ✛ *Near the California Lighthouse.*

Casibari and Ayo Rock Formations

NATURE SIGHT | The odd-looking massive boulders at Ayo and Casibari are a mystery, as they don't match the island's geological makeup in any other spot. They seem to have just cropped up out of nowhere, but they're cool to see. Casibari is fun to climb with man-made steps, handrails, and tunnels set within the weird rock formation. Kids will love this all-natural jungle gym. You are not permitted to climb Ayo, but it's still worth a visit to see the ancient pictographs in its small cave (the entrance has iron bars to protect the drawings from vandalism). ⊕ *www.aruba.com/us/explore/rock-formations.*

★ Donkey Sanctuary Aruba

FARM/RANCH | FAMILY | Take a free tour of the island's only donkey sanctuary where volunteers help abandoned and sometimes ill wild animals enjoy a happy forever home. This is a nonprofit organization and can always use help, whether financially or with chores. You can donate there or on their website, and you can even adopt a donkey—your donation goes to its annual feed and care. There is also a great donkey-themed gift shop. It's a great family outing for all ages. Bring apples and carrots if you want to make fast friends with the residents. ∎TIP➜ **For any donation, you can have a one-on-one hugging session with a donkey for 30 minutes. It's a great stress reliever.** ⊠ *Bringamosa, Bringamosa 2Z, Santa Cruz* ☎ *297/593–2933* ⊕ *main.arubandonkey.org/portal* 🖾 *Free.*

Mt. Hooiberg

MOUNTAIN | Named for its shape (hooiberg means "haystack" in Dutch), this 541-foot peak lies inland, just past the airport. You are bound to notice it as your plane lands. If you have the energy, you can climb the 562 steps to the top for an impressive view of Oranjestad (and Venezuela on clear days). It is the island's second-highest peak; Mt. Jamanota is the tallest at 617 feet. ∎TIP➜ **It's a very hot climb with no shade, so wear a hat, apply plenty of sunscreen, and bring water.** ⊠ *Hooiberg 11, Paradera* ✛ *Near Santa Cruz.*

7

★ Studio Murano Art

ART GALLERY | This large, beautifully restored *cunucu* house offers daily glassblowing exhibitions by a master artisan from the island of Murano, Italy, famous for its glass art. Also on the property is a large bar/restaurant with a very interesting and eclectic choice of international fare. It's an odd combination but it really works, and it's become a popular stop for groups doing island tours. Watch free daily glassblowing presentations between 11 am and 1 pm, and shop for original souvenirs on-site; you can also book a workshop to make your own glass art souvenir. ⊠ *Ayo 22, Santa Cruz* ☎ *297/584–8148* ⊕ *studiomuranoart.com* 🎫 *Free*.

☕ Coffee and Quick Bites

The interior neighborhoods of Santa Cruz (before you enter the park) and Paradera nearby are full of little snack bars, food trucks, cafés, small restaurants, and bakeries, so seek them out for an authentic local experience while you explore another side of Aruba.

★ Bright Bakery

$ | **CAFÉ** | This landmark family-run bakery has been a local favorite since it first opened in 1949, and it's still home to the island's most authentic baked goods, including epic cakes, cupcakes, and pastries. There are also sandwiches and savory snacks like *pastechi* (handheld stuffed pastries) and hot dog *broodjes* ideal for a grab-and-go lunch or breakfast. **Known for:** the largest collection of authentic Aruban cakes; wonderful homemade breads and buns; a cheery spot for breakfast. **⑤** *Average main: $10* ⊠ *Piedra Plat 44, Paradera* ☎ *297/585–9031* ⊕ *www.facebook.com/ brightbakeryaruba*.

★ Huchada Bakery

$$ | **BAKERY** | Located about five minutes from Arikok National Park's entrance, this spot has always been a legendary place for authentic Aruban baked goods, especially whole *bolos* (cakes). They still have about 20 kinds to choose from, including a few 6-inch sizes. **Known for:** local bolos and pastries; great homemade soups and stews; local specialties. **⑤** *Average main: $12* ⊠ *Santa Cruz 328, Santa Cruz* ☎ *297/585–8302* ⊕ *www.facebook.com/ Huchadaonline*.

Did You Know?

Scientists don't know the geological origins of the massive Casibari and Ayo rock formations. Locals jokingly say aliens dropped them here. There are staircases to aid in exploring them.

The Lionfish Snack

$$ | CARIBBEAN | "Eat 'em to beat 'em" is the motto behind this snack shack that serves only lionfish dishes—deep-fried lionfish, sandwiches, wraps, smoked fillets, and a lionfish dip—to help combat the invasive species. It's only open Saturdays from noon to 7:30 pm, so make sure to plan accordingly if you really want to eat here. **Known for:** lionfish fritters; lionfish wings; lionfish wraps. ⑤ *Average main: $12 ⊠ Paradera 100, Paradera ⊕ thelionfishsnack-aruba.com ⊟ No credit cards ⊗ Closed Sun.–Fri.*

★ Urataka Center / Best Pizza

$$ | BRASSERIE | As the name suggests, this is a local favorite for pizza in Santa Cruz, but they also serve great snack platters, chicken, and burgers. There's outdoor garden seating and cold beer on tap, too. **Known for:** specialty and create-your-own pizzas; chicken wing baskets; superb burgers. ⑤ *Average main: $12 ⊠ Urataka 12A, Santa Cruz ☎ 297/585–5212 ⊕ www.facebook. com/UratakaCenter.*

ACTIVITIES

Updated by
Susan Campbell

On Aruba, you can hike or bike a surreal arid outback and participate in every conceivable water sport, play tennis or golf, and go horseback riding along the sea. The island has also become the beach tennis capital of the Caribbean, so do give it a try while you're here. Snorkeling and diving are big, of course, but there's also parasailing, banana boats, kayaking, paddleboarding—even yoga on a paddleboard—touring submarines, luxury sails, golf, and skydiving.

Aruba has many fitness clubs that visitors are welcome to join, too. And there's a novel way to enjoy Aruba's abundant nature in style, with a custom luxury setup of gourmet fare and outdoor comfort provided by Picnic Aruba (⊕ *www.picnicaruba.com*), the island's only licensed and official picnic company.

The island's constant trade winds make it an ideal place to learn to windsurf, kiteboard, and wing foil.

Biking and Motorcycling

Cycling is a great way to get around the island—though biking along busy roads is not encouraged. Linear Park's paved trail from Downtown Oranjestad to the airport or from Fisherman's Huts Beach to Malmok is ideal for families seeking a biking adventure along the sea. Green Bike kiosks dot the island, making it easy to grab a bike and deposit it at another station when you're done. If you'd rather cycle with less exertion, there are electric bike rentals, too. Many resorts offer their guests coaster bikes or e-bikes for free (or for a low fee) to pedal around the beach areas, and there are also guided mountain bike tours that take you into the rugged interior. Or let your hair down completely and cruise around on a Harley-Davidson, either solo or with a group tour.

Relatively flat, Aruba can be the perfect biking destination.

Rentals

★ George's Cycles Co.

FOUR-WHEELING | This outfit has been renting motorcycles, scooters, and ATVs since the late 1980s. It's a reputable firm that offers great vehicles at good prices. Hotel pickup and drop-off options are available. For private and elite customized VIP island adventures, try their sister company Aruba Cine Tours (⊕ *www.arubacinetours.com*). ⊠ *L. G. Smith Blvd. 124, Oranjestad* ☎ *297/594–0245* ⊕ *www.georgecycle.com* ✉ *From $55 per day.*

★ Green Bike Aruba

BIKING | It's no surprise that the first bike-sharing program in the Caribbean quickly became popular, since Aruba is a Dutch-influenced island and people from the Netherlands adore their bikes. With more than 100 modern bikes at 8 docking stations dotting the island (at busy tourist junctions, including the cruise terminal), it's easy to swipe your credit card and hit the road or download the Green app for easy QR code operation. There's also a growing network of app-operated e-scooters. ⊠ *Caya Ernesto Petronia Ponton 69, Oranjestad* ☎ *297/594–6368* ⊕ *greenbikearuba.com* ✉ *From $15 (2 hours).*

Organized Excursions

★ Aruba Active Vacations Mountain Biking Tours

BIKING | Unless you are a skilled cyclist, it's best to join a tour to explore the island's arid, rugged, and unforgiving outback. This outfitter offers 2-hour guided tours and private tours on top-quality Cannondale bikes with water and helmets supplied. Points of interest include Alto Vista Chapel and the California Lighthouse, and the tour begins at the company's windsurfing shop at Fisherman's Huts. You can also rent the Cannondale bikes on your own. Guests must be at least 16 years to participate. ⊠ *Fisherman's Huts Beach, Malmokweg* ☎ *297/586–0989* ⊕ *aruba-active-vacations.com* ⊠ *From $60 (minimum 2 people).*

Bird-Watching

★ Birdwatching Aruba

BIRD WATCHING | This intimate outfit is run by Michiel Oversteegen, an award-winning professional wildlife photographer who can arrange private birding or nature photo tours with photo instruction as well. Tours are good for beginning birders as well as the most avid ornithologist, or anyone who wants to discover the island's surprisingly eclectic and abundant selection of birds. Bubali Bird Sanctuary is a popular place to add to your life list if you're an avid birder. ■**TIP**→ **Pickup and drop-off are included, but a max of five people are allowed with a minimum of four hours; online booking only.** ⊠ *Bubali, Oranjestad* ☎ *297/699–2075* ⊕ *www.birdwatchingaruba.com.*

Bowling

★ Dream Bowl Aruba

BOWLING | **FAMILY** | Perfect for all ages, Dream Bowl does it right with eight glow-in-the-dark bowling lanes, hip music, computerized scoring, a video arcade, a food court, a bar, and prize machines. ■**TIP**→ **The bowling alley is open after 4 pm on weekends and after 5 pm on weekdays.** ⊠ *Palm Beach Plaza, L. G. Smith Blvd. 95, Suite 310, Palm Beach* ☎ *297/280–8888* ⊕ *www.facebook.com/Dreambowl* ⊠ *From $22* ⊙ *Closed Thurs.*

Eagle Bowling Palace

BOWLING | **FAMILY** | Arubans love to bowl and often compete off-island. The Eagle emporium is the local favorite spot. Close to the high-rise strip, it has computerized lanes, a snack bar, a cocktail lounge, and occasional big screen bingo. Equipment rentals and group rates are available. It opens after 3 pm. ⊠ *Pos Abao 2N, Pos Abao* ☎ *297/583–5038* ⊕ *www.facebook.com/eagle.bowling.9* ⚏ *From $20 per lane per hour* ☾ *Closed Mon.*

Day Sails

Aruba is not much of a sailing destination—the marina is tiny by many Caribbean island standards—but they are big on luxury catamarans taking large groups out for a fun day of party sailing, snorkeling tours, or sunset dinner cruises. The weather is typically ideal, the waters are calm and clear, and the trade winds are gentle, so there's never really a bad time to hit the waves.

The main operators are DePalm, Red Sail, and Pelican. All have large catamarans, but some companies like Jolly Pirates and Sail Away also offer old-fashioned wooden schooners for their day sails and snorkeling trips. A few smaller private yacht charters are available as well. Many tours make stops for snorkeling and often include drinks, snacks, loud music, and sometimes even romantic, adult-only sunset dinners.

Day sails usually take off from either DePalm Pier, Hadicurari Pier, or Pelican Pier on Palm Beach. Many tour companies include pickup and drop-off services at major resorts that are not on Palm Beach.

★ Jolly Pirates
SNORKELING | FAMILY | Aruba's unique pirate-themed sailing adventure is a rollicking ride aboard a big beautiful teak schooner, complete with a wild and crazy swashbuckling crew and an open bar. The ships offer snorkeling tours with two or three snorkeling stops and a rope-swing adventure, and the sunset cruises are also first-rate. Prepare to party hearty (it's basically impossible not to) due to their signature "pirate's poison" rum punch and infectious loud music. Snorkel stops always include the *Antilla* wreck. The new "Grub and Grog" adventure also includes a bountiful BBQ, and there's an adults-only Thursday version. Departures are from Hadicurari Pier beside MooMba Beach Bar. ⊠ *Hadicurari Pier, Palm Beach* ⊹ *Office behind MooMba Beach Bar* ☎ *297/586–8107* ⊕ *www.jolly-pirates.com* ⚏ *From $45 (sunset sail) and $69 (snorkel sail).*

★ Montforte III
SAILING | Take your sailing experience up a notch aboard this luxurious teak schooner that is designed to pamper. Exclusive tours take you to spots like Spanish Lagoon for snorkeling and kayaking,

Snorkeling from a replica pirate ship will thrill any swashbuckler.

and around Boca Catalina for four-course dinners under the stars. Unlimited premium spirits, signature cocktails, tapas, and snacks are included in all trips, and there's sometimes live music onboard as well. Departure is from Pelican Pier. All cruises are adults-only. ✉ *Pelican Pier, Palm Beach* ☎ *297/583–0400* ⊕ *monfortecruise. com* ✉ *From $139.*

★ Octopus Aruba

SAILING | Octopus has been offering group and private snorkel and party sails on their catamaran for decades, but now they also offer unique experiences with a fleet of cool "aqua donut" boats. The donuts seat up to 10 people on a comfy padded bench circling a large table; you can captain it yourself or have it crewed. Stable and easy to navigate, the aqua donut won't sink even if it's full of water. Octopus offers two very cool catered adventures aboard them—a luxury brunch and snorkel outing, and a gourmet dinner sunset cruise. It's like having your own table and floating bar on the sea, but they call it your own "private island." ✉ *Palm Beach* ⊹ *Orange beach hut between the Playa Linda and Holiday Inn* ☎ *297/560–6565* ⊕ *octopusaruba.com* ✉ *From $69.99.*

Sailaway Tours Aruba

SAILING | **FAMILY** | At 110 feet, the *Lady Black* is a beautifully retrofitted old-fashioned wooden schooner that's also the island's largest party ship. Enjoy an open bar and a big rope hammock on the bow while you sail with one of their snorkel, sunset, or dinner cruises. The friendly crew is happy to help you try some antics on the rope swing, and you can even hop on their backs while they do flips into the water. The party can get crazy. Private charters are available, as are land and sea tours. ⊠ *Hadicurari Pier, Palm Beach* ⚓ *Look for their sign to check in across from MooMba Beach Bar in front of Hadicurari Pier* ☎ *297/732–3000* ⊕ *sailawaytour.com* 🖃 *From $70 (Weekend specials $50).*

★ Tranquilo Charters Aruba

SAILING | Captain Mike Hagedoorn, a legendary Aruban sailor, handed the helm over to his son Captain Anthony a few years ago after 20 years of running the family business. Today, the *Tranquilo*—a 43-foot sailing yacht—still takes small groups of passengers to a secluded spot at a Spanish lagoon named Mike's Reef, where not many other snorkel trips venture. The lunch cruise to the south side always includes "Mom's famous Dutch pea soup," and they also do private charters for romantic dinner sails and sailing trips around Aruba's lesser-explored coasts. Look for the red boat docked at the Renaissance Marina beside the Atlantis Submarine launch. ⊠ *Renaissance Marina, Oranjestad* ☎ *297/586–1418* ⊕ *www.tranquiloaruba.com* 🖃 *From $100.*

Fishing

Deep-sea catches here include anything from barracuda, tuna, and wahoo to kingfish, sailfish, and marlins. A few skippered charter boats are available for half- or full-day excursions. Package prices vary but typically include tackle, bait, and refreshments. A few restaurants will cook your fresh catch for your dinner, too.

★ Driftwood Charters

FISHING | Driftwood is a tournament-rigged 35-foot yacht manned by Captain Herby, who is famous for offering deep-sea fishing charters on Aruba since the early 1990s. He is also co-owner of Driftwood Restaurant and is always happy to bring your catch to their chef for expert preparation, so you can enjoy it for dinner the very same night. Charters can accommodate up to six people. ⊠ *Renaissance Marina, Oranjestad* ☎ *297/592–4040* ⊕ *www. driftwoodfishingcharters.com* 🖃 *From $480.*

Teaser Fishing Charters Aruba

FISHING | **FAMILY** | The expertise of the Teaser crew is matched by a commitment to sensible fishing practices, which include catch and release and avoiding ecologically sensitive areas. The company's 35-foot Bertram sport fisher yacht is fully equipped, and the crew seem to have an uncanny ability to locate the best fishing spots with Captain Milton at the helm. Maximum six people.

There are a number of operators that offer tours on horseback.

✉ *Renaissance Marina, Oranjestad* ☎ *297/593–9228* ⊕ *teaser-fishingaruba.com* 🖃 *From $480.*

Golf

There are two very different courses to enjoy on Aruba.

The Links at Divi Aruba

GOLF | This 9-hole course is the focal point of the Divi Village Golf and Beach Resort. Designed by Karl Litten and Lorie Viola, the par-36 flat layout stretches to 2,952 yards, featuring paspalum grass (best for seaside courses) and taking you past beautiful lagoons full of seabirds and nature. It's a testy little course with water abounding, making accuracy more important than distance. Amenities include a golf school with professional instruction, a driving range, a practice green, and a two-story golf clubhouse with a pro shop. It's open to the public, but resort guests receive preferred tee times. ✉ *Divi Village Golf and Beach Resort, J. E. Irausquin Blvd. 93, Druif* ☎ *297/581–4653* ⊕ *divilinks.com* 🖃 *From $97; $81 after 3 pm* 🏌 *9 holes, 2952 yards, par 36.*

★ Tierra del Sol

GOLF | Stretching out to 6,811 yards, this stunning course is situated on the northwest coast near the California Lighthouse and is Aruba's only 18-hole course. Designed by Robert Trent Jones Jr., Tierra del Sol combines Aruba's native beauty (cacti and rock formations, stunning views) with good greens and beautiful landscaping. Wind can also be a factor here on the rolling terrain, as are the abundant bunkers and water hazards. Greens fees include a golf cart equipped with GPS and a communications system that allows you to order drinks for your return to the clubhouse. The club also offers clinics and lessons and hosts many major tournament and gala golf events annually. ⊠ *Tierra del Sol Resort, Caya di Solo 10* ☎ *297/586–7800* ⊕ *www.tierradelsol.com/ golf* 🗺 *From $89 for 9 holes (high season)* 🎍. *18 holes, 6811 yards, par 71.*

Hiking

Despite Aruba's arid landscape, hiking the rugged countryside will give you the best opportunities to see the island's wildlife and flora; guides are highly recommended for those with little hiking experience. Arikok National Park is an excellent place to glimpse the real Aruba, free of the trappings of tourism. The heat can be oppressive though, so be sure to go early in the day, wear a hat, and have a refillable bottle of water handy as there are no places to dispose of plastic bottles. Get maps and information at Arikok National Park Visitor Center.

Beyond Arikok National Park, the 500-step trek up Mt. Hooiberg (locals call it "The Haystack") is also a good workout that rewards with fabulous island views.

★ Arikok National Park

HIKING & WALKING | There are more than 20 miles of trails concentrated in the island's eastern interior and along its northeastern . coast. Arikok Park is crowned by Aruba's second-highest mountain, the 577-foot Mt. Arikok, so you can also go climbing there. Hiking in the park, whether alone or in a group led by guides, is generally not too strenuous, but it is hot. You'll need sturdy shoes to grip the granular surfaces and climb the occasionally steep terrain. You should also exercise caution with the strong sun—bring along plenty of water and wear sunscreen and a hat. At the park's main entrance, the Arikok Visitor Center houses exhibits, restrooms, and snack concessions and provides maps and information about marked trails, park rules, and features. Free guided mini tours are the best way to get oriented at the park entrance. You can also download hiking maps from their website for self-guided tours. ☎ *297/585–1234* ⊕ *www.arubanationalpark. org* 🗺 *$15 park entrance, $50 annual pass* 🕙 *Park closes at 4 pm* ☞ *Last entrance tickets sold at 3:30 pm.*

Horseback Riding

Ranches offer short jaunts along the beach or longer rides through the countryside and even to the ruins of an old gold mill. Riders of all experience levels will be thrilled that most of Aruba's horses are descendants of the Spanish Paso Fino—meaning "fine step"—which offer a super smooth ride even at a trot. Be sure to ask for one if you take a trail ride.

★ Gold Mine Ranch

HORSEBACK RIDING | A family-run operation spanning five generations, what began as an animal rescue ranch has become a tour company with a focus on the ultimate nature adventures and a healthy relationship between horse and rider. Some of the gorgeous vistas encountered include a hidden valley and lagoon and a secret land bridge, as well as the ruins of the old gold mine. There may also be an exhilarating beach ride. Private tours are available, as are complimentary pickup and drop-off in the main hotel areas. ⊠ *Matividiri 60, Paradera* ☎ *287/585–9870* ⊕ *www. thegoldmineranch.com* 🖭 *From $98.*

★ Hoofs of Hope

HORSEBACK RIDING | Providing guided horseback rides through Arikok National Park and some beachside treks, this outfit is all about personal service. Sunset, sunrise, and day trips are available, as are private tours. The organization is committed to re-homing the island's rescue horses, and it's involved in "hippotherapy," a service provided to the island's local children with special needs that involves bonding with the animals. ⊠ *Safir 65Z, Westpunt* ☎ *213/510–0822* ⊕ *www.hoofsofhope.org* 🖭 *From $85.*

Rancho Loco

HORSEBACK RIDING | **FAMILY** | Surrounded by a lush fruit and vegetable farm, Rancho Loco is touted as the "greenest ranch in Aruba." This equestrian center also gives lessons and boards and trains horses. Their tours range from sunset jaunts on Moro Beach to Arikok National Park interior treks, including trips to the Conchi. Private rides are also available. ⊠ *Sombre 22E, Santa Cruz* ☎ *297/592–6039* ⊕ *www.rancholocoaruba.com/en* 🖭 *From $95.*

★ Rancho La Ponderosa

HORSEBACK RIDING | **FAMILY** | Discover the wild pristine north coast on horseback and visit secret Wariruri Beach for a gallop along the sea. Small group or private tours are available mornings and afternoons, and special private packages including a picnic in nature, a photoshoot, and other special add-ons can be arranged. They only use Paso Fino horses, known for their exceptionally smooth gait.

The calm waters and mangrove lagoons found along Aruba's southern coast around Mangel Halto are ideal for kayaking.

Complimentary pickup and drop-off is provided at major hotels. ✉ *Papaya 30, Paradera* ☎ *297/594–8884* ⊕ *horsebackridingaruba. com* 💰 *From $105* 🕐 *Closed Sun.* ☞ *Children must be over 6 years old to ride their own horse.*

Jet Skiing

There are a few spots to book Jet Skis or WaveRunners along Palm Beach, including the family-run full-service water sports outfitter, Aruba Watersports Center (⇨ *see Recommended Dive Operators under Scuba Diving and Snorkeling*).

Kayaking

Kayaking is a popular sport on Aruba, especially because the waters are so calm. It's a great way to explore the coast and the mangroves. Clear-bottom kayaks are available, as are completely translucent kayaks.

Aruba Outdoor Adventures

KAYAKING | This small family-run outfitter offers a unique combination of small-group (six people max) pedal-kayaking and snorkel tours along the island's southeastern coast. Mangroves and reef explorations take you around calm water near Mangel Halto, Savaneta, and Barcadera; well-informed guides explain the natural environment and help guests navigate the snorkeling portions. No kayaking experience is necessary. Pickup and drop-off are included, as well as snorkel equipment, a dry bag, snacks, and drinks. Departures are from the De Palm Island Ferry Terminal outside Oranjestad. ⊠ *DePalm Island Ferry Terminal, Balashi* ☎ *297/749–6646* ⊕ *www.arubaoutdooradventures.com* ⊠ *From $60.*

★ Clear Kayak Aruba

KAYAKING | FAMILY | This is the first Aruba outfitter to offer clear-bottom sea kayaks, and the only one offering night tours. By day, groups paddle through the natural mangroves at Mangel Halto with a guide who can tell you how the roots create a natural nursery for juvenile marine life; the route also passes over lots of big healthy coral full of colorful tropical fish. A second tour begins at Arashi Beach at dusk; then, after dark, the kayaks are lit up with LED lights that attract marine life to their clear bottoms. Pickup and drop-off are available for an extra charge. ⊠ *Savaneta 402, Savaneta* ☎ *297/566–2205* ⊕ *clearkayakaruba.com* ⊠ *From $65* ⊗ *Closed Mon.* ☞ *Children must be age 8 and over for day tours and 12 and over for night tours.*

Multisport Outfitters

There are a number of outfitters in Aruba that can handle nearly all of your water- or land-based activities with guided excursions and rental equipment. Here is a list of a few of our favorites.

Around Aruba Tours

SPECIAL-INTEREST TOURS | Spearheaded by Philip Merryweather, owner of Philip's Animal Garden, this tour operator likes to do things a little differently, focusing on education and eco-conservation as much as possible while still offering adrenaline-rush explorations in a variety of vehicles; they promise to bring you to the island's best hidden natural gems and vistas. They also offer private luxury boat and catamaran tours, as well as UTV, ATV, Surrey bikes, and Jet Ski rentals. ⊠ *Alto Vista 116, Noord* ☎ *297/593–6363* ⊕ *www.aroundarubatours.com* ⊠ *From $60.*

★ Aruba Nature Explorers

ECOTOURISM | The most eco-friendly way to explore the island's nature and enchanting secret spots is with this outfitter's unique themed tours like the sunrise hike and beach meditation at Alto Vista or mangrove hiking and kayaking through Spanish Lagoon. There's also a tour that teaches guests about Aruba's surprising gold rush history with an enlightening guided hike through Bushiribana. But their most mindful and exhilarating trek is a private guided hike through Arikok National Park that culminates in a snorkel dip in the famous Conchi natural pool. They also do bird-watching tours, VIP private island tours, and private boat charters. ■TIP→ **Many tours include breakfast or lunch in the price.** ✉ *Orange Plaza, Engelanstraat 2, Unit 7, Oranjestad* ☎ *297/731–0077* ⊕ *arubaeco.tours* ✈ *From $95.*

★ De Palm Tours

SPECIAL-INTEREST TOURS | FAMILY | Aruba's premier tour company covers every inch of the island on land and undersea, and they even have their own submarine (Atlantis) and semi-submarine (*Seaworld Explorer*). Their all-inclusive private island destination (De Palm Island) has great snorkeling, its own flock of flamingos, and Seatrek, a cool underwater air-supplied helmet walk. Land exploration options include air-conditioned bus sightseeing tours, jeep safaris to popular attractions like the Conchi natural pool, and off-road tours in a UTV. On the water, their luxury catamaran *De Palm Pleasure* offers sunset sails and snorkel trips that include an option to try SNUBA—deeper snorkeling with an air-supplied raft at Aruba's most famous shipwreck. De Palm also offers airport transfers and private VIP transfers. ✉ *L. G. Smith Blvd. 142, Oranjestad* ☎ *297/522–4400* ⊕ *depalm.com.*

EL Tours

SPECIAL-INTEREST TOURS | This outfit offers an eclectic range of island tours including Aruba highlights; beach hopping with snorkeling ops; a fauna tour visiting the island's best animal sanctuaries; hiking tours with a park ranger in Arikok National Park; and morning and afternoon off-roading options. Private tours are also available. The range of vehicles includes air-conditioned and open-air buses, jeeps, and UTVs. They also offer a wide range of airport transfer services, including VIP luxury options. ✉ *Opal 58, Noord, Oranjestad* ☎ *297/585–6730* ⊕ *www.eltoursaruba.com* ✈ *Tours from $41.*

Pelican Adventures

SAILING | FAMILY | This family-owned tour and water sports company in operation since 1984 is now one of the island's largest activity hubs; they've also partnered with some of the island's smaller operators to offer every conceivable way to explore this island on land and sea. They also have their own dedicated pier and Pelican Nest bar/restaurant on Palm Beach, an ideal spot for dinner or drinks after an outing. ✉ *Pelican Pier, J. E. Irausquin Blvd 237, Noord* ☎ *297/587–2302* ⊕ *www.pelican-aruba.com* ✈ *From $53.*

Red Sail Sports Aruba

BOATING | A dynamic company established in 1989, they are experts in the field of water-sports recreation. They offer excellent diving excursions and instruction, snorkel sails, sunset sails, and

Aruba is known as the wreck diving capital of the Caribbean.

full dinner sails. The company also has its own sports equipment shops, and you can also book many land excursions through them. Special day-tripping land and sea packages are available for cruise ship passengers. They also offer deep-sea fishing charters. ✉ *Palm Beach, Opal 58, Palm Beach* ☎ *297/523–1600* ⊕ *www. redsailaruba.com.*

Parasailing

This incredible overwater adventure, which typically lasts for 15 minutes, will make you feel as free as a bird. Single or tandem trips are available departing from Palm Beach. Aruba Watersports Center is a best bet for first-timers. (■ **TIP→ See Recommended Dive Operators under Scuba Diving and Snorkeling**).

Scuba Diving and Snorkeling

With visibility of up to 90 feet, the clear waters around Aruba are excellent for snorkeling and diving. In fact, Aruba is known as one of the wreck-diving capitals of the Caribbean. Advanced and novice divers alike will find plenty to occupy their time, as many of the most popular sites—including some interesting shipwrecks—are found in shallow waters ranging from 30 to 60 feet. Coral reefs covered with sensuously waving sea fans and eerie giant sponge tubes attract a colorful menagerie of sea life, including gliding manta rays, curious sea turtles, shy octopuses, and fish from grunts to groupers. Marine preservation is a priority on Aruba, and regulations by the Conference on International Trade in Endangered Species make it unlawful to remove coral, conch, and other marine life from the water. Using only reef-safe sunscreen is now also a law.

Day-sail operators often offer snorkeling, and it's usually coupled with an open bar and loud music; almost all of them stop at the famous *Antilla* shipwreck just offshore, which provides a rare treat for snorkelers to be able to view a wreck typically only divers would be able to access. Some dive operators also allow snorkelers to tag along with divers on a trip for a lower fee as well.

Major West-Side Dive Sites

Airplane Wrecks. Two planes purposely scuttled to create a dive site are still somewhat intact around Renaissance Private Island. You must do a drift dive to see them; they broke apart somewhat after Hurricane Lenny caused big swells in the area back in 1999.

Antilla **Wreck.** This German freighter, which sank off the northwest coast near Malmok Beach, is popular with both divers and snorkelers. Some outfits also offer SNUBA, which allows you to get a bit closer to the wreck if you are not certified to dive. When Germany declared war on the Netherlands in 1940 during World War II, it was stationed off the coast. The captain chose to sink the ship on purpose before Aruban officials could board and seize it. The 400-foot-long vessel—referred to by locals as "the ghost ship"—broke into two distinct halves. It has large compartments, and you can climb into the captain's bathtub, which sits beside the wreck, for a unique photo op. Lobster, angelfish, yellowtail, and other fish swim about the wreck, which is blanketed by giant tube sponges and coral.

Blackstone Beach. The clear waters just off this beach are dotted with sea fans. The area takes its name from the rounded black stones lining the shore. It's the only bay on the island's north coast sheltered from thunderous waves, making it a safe spot for diving, though currents are very strong, so it's recommended for experienced divers only.

California **Wreck.** Although this steamer is submerged at a depth that's perfect for underwater photography, this site is safe only for advanced divers; the currents here are strong, and the waters are dangerously choppy. This wreck is what the famous lighthouse is named for.

Malmok Reef (*Debbie II* **Wreck).** Lobsters and stingrays are among the highlights at this bottom reef adorned by giant green, orange, and purple barrel sponges as well as leaf and brain coral. From here you can spot the *Debbie II*, a 120-foot barge that sank in 1992.

Pedernales **Wreck.** During World War II, this oil tanker was torpedoed by a German submarine. The U.S. military cut out the damaged centerpiece, towed the two remaining pieces to the States, and welded them together into a smaller vessel that eventually transported troops during the invasion of Normandy. The section that was left behind in shallow water is now surrounded by coral formations, making this a good site for novice divers. The ship's cabins, washbasins, and pipelines are exposed. The area teems with grouper and angelfish. It's also a good site for snorkelers since it's easily visible from the shallows, and you can even see it from above when you parasail over it just off of Palm Beach.

Tugboat Wreck. Spotted eagle rays and stingrays are sometimes observed at this shipwreck at the foot of Harbour Reef, which is one of Aruba's most popular. Spectacular formations of brain, sheet, and star coral blanket the path to the wreck, which is inhabited by several bright-green moray eels.

East-Side Dive Sites

Jane C. Wreck. This 200-foot freighter, lodged in an almost vertical position at a depth of 90 feet, is near the coral reef west of De Palm Island. Night diving is exciting here, as the polyps emerge from the corals that grow profusely on the steel plates of the decks and cabins. Soft corals and sea fans are also abundant in the area. The current is strong, and this is for advanced divers only.

Punta Basora. This narrow reef stretches far into the sea off the island's easternmost point. On calm days you'll see eagle rays, stingrays, barracudas, and hammerhead sharks, as well as hawksbill and loggerhead turtles.

The Wall. From May to August, green sea turtles intent on laying their eggs abound at this steep-walled reef. You'll also spot groupers and burrfish swimming nearby. Close to shore, massive sheet corals are plentiful; in the upper part of the reef are colorful varieties such as black coral, star coral, and flower coral. Flitting about are brilliant damselfish, rock beauties, and porgies.

Recommended Dive Operators

★ Aruba Watersports Center

DIVING & SNORKELING | FAMILY | This family-run full-service water sports outfitter right on Palm Beach offers a variety of water-based adventures including snorkeling trips, but it's their small on-site dive center that attracts those seeking personalized underwater explorations with personable certified experts. Small group PADI dives to nearby wrecks are popular, and they also offer excellent instruction for first-timers with their Discover Scuba courses. Refresher PADI courses are also available. They also rent tanks and gear. ⊠ *L. G. Smith Blvd. 81B, Palm Beach* ⊹ *Between Barceló and Hilton resorts* ☎ *297/586–6613* ⊕ *arubawatersportscenter.com* ⊠ *Dives from $107.*

★ De Palm Pleasure Sail & Snorkeling

SNORKELING | FAMILY | The luxury catamaran *De Palm Pleasure* offers three-stop snorkel trips to the island's most popular fish-filled spots daily, including the *Antilla* shipwreck. They also offer the option to try SNUBA. The romantic sunset sails are popular excursions. Buffet and open bar are included. Hotel pickup and drop-off are also included (unless within easy walking distance of their pier on Palm Beach). ⊠ *De Palm Pier, Palm Beach* ⊹ *Between the Hilton and the Riu resorts* ☎ *297/522–4400* ⊕ *depalm. com* ⊠ *From $69.*

★ JADS Dive Center

SCUBA DIVING | Owned by the local Fang family, JADS has been in operation for decades and is famous for its "Discover Scuba" package that takes you to one of the island's only shore-diving sites at Mangel Halto, which has easy access for beginners. JADS also offers all levels of PADI dive instruction, a children's program, personalized boat dive trips, and guided night dives. Located right on Baby Beach, they operate a full-service dive shop with snorkel equipment rentals. Rum Reef, an adult-only infinity pool bar also owned by the family, is right next door. ■**TIP→ Looking for a unique souvenir? One dive instructor sells handmade jewelry made from lion-fish skin in the dive shop; the craft helps rid the environment of these destructive fish.** ⊠ *Seroe Colorado 245E, San Nicolaas* ☎ *297/584–6070* ⊕ *jadsaruba.com* ⊠ *From $58* ⊝ *Closed Sun.*

Native Divers Aruba

SCUBA DIVING | A small personal operation, Native Divers Aruba specializes in PADI open-water courses. Ten different certification options include specialties like Multilevel Diver, Search and Recovery Diver, and Underwater Naturalist. Their boat schedule is also flexible, and it's easy to tailor instruction to your specific needs. They allow snorkelers to tag along and provide all the necessary equipment, and they offer resort classes and refresher courses. ⊠ *Marriott Surf Club, Palm Beach* ✛ *On the beach in front of Marriott Surf Club* ☎ *297/586–4763* ⊕ *www.nativedivers. com* ⊠ *From $80.*

S.E. Aruba Fly 'n Dive

SCUBA DIVING | One of the island's oldest diving operators, S.E. Aruba Fly 'n Dive offers a full range of PADI courses as well as many specialty courses like Nitrox Diver, Wreck Diver, and Deep Diver. Private snorkeling trips are available, and they can also instruct you in rescue techniques, becoming an underwater naturalist, or underwater photography. Night dives on request (minimum of four divers). ⊠ *Bucutiweg 20, Oranjestad* ☎ *297/588–1150* ⊕ *se-aruba. com* ⊠ *From $95.*

Skydiving

★ SkyDive Aruba

SKYDIVING | There's nothing like the adrenaline rush when you are forced to jump out of a perfectly good airplane at 10,000 feet because you are attached to your instructor. You have no choice but to free-fall at 120 mph toward the island for 35 seconds until your chute opens, and then your downward journey has you floating to the sand in a little over five minutes. Afterward you can purchase a video of your courageous leap. Group discounts are available. Hotel pickup and drop-off are included. ⊠ *Malmok Beach, Malmokweg* ☎ *297/735–0654* ⊕ *skydivearuba.com* ⊠ *From $299* ☞ *Minimum age is 13 and the minimum weight is 100 lbs.*

Spas

Aruba Floating Spa

SPAS | Few things are as rejuvenating as a professional massage— except maybe receiving one while the sway of the sea lulls you into an even deeper mode of euphoria. New to the island, this unique concept takes place on a canopied raft tethered approximately 20 feet from land in Governor's Bay. Patrons are transported by boat to the platform, where therapists await to work their magic. Treatment choices include relaxation, therapeutic, or deep-tissue massages; add-ons of extra time on a separate raft afterward with Champagne and charcuterie are also available. ■**TIP**➔ **There are no changing facilities on board; see their website for preferred attire before treatments.** ⊠ *Governor's Bay, Oranjestad*

⚓ *Pickup for the boat to the raft is in the parking lot behind the West Deck Grill* ☎ *297/699–9039* ⊕ *arubafloatingmassage.com* ✉ *From $250* ⊘ *Closed Sun.*

eforea Spa

SPAS | Hilton's answer to Zen incarnate, this soothing white seafront building beckons you to enter a world of relaxing signature "journeys" in a Japanese-inspired enclave. Treatments include both the typical and avant-garde, and there are options for both women and men, as well as special beachfront massages for couples. There's also a stellar water circuit and full-service beauty salon on-site. Their signature massage includes Aruban aloe and local rum, and they also feature a massage with sound vibrational therapy. ✉ *Hilton Aruba Caribbean Resort and Casino, J. E. Irausquin Blvd. 81, Palm Beach* ☎ *297/526–6052* ⊕ *www.hilton. com/en/hotels/auahhhh-hilton-aruba-caribbean-resort-and-casino/ things-to-do/spa/.*

★ Indira Skincare

SPAS | An enchanting surprise awaits on the road to San Nicolas, just before the Savaneta turnoff, in the form of this full-service spa and art gallery owned by artist Merveline Geerman, who also happens to be a licensed skin-care specialist and masseuse. A full range of treatments are available, including makeup and mani-pedis. ✉ *Savaneta 91, Savaneta* ☎ *297/584–6263* ⊕ *facebook. com/IndiraSkincareAruba* ⊘ *Closed Sun.*

★ Indulgence by the Sea

SPAS | The spa-salon serving Divi Aruba and Tamarijn all-inclusives offers a wide range of premium services, but it's split into two locations. The salon that offers professional hair and nail care is located at Tamarijn Resort in a beautifully renovated glassed-in venue; it's very popular for specialty makeup and wedding hair. The spa portion is at Divi Aruba, offering a full menu of facials, massages, and luxurious body treatments. All products are hand-picked and tested by the owner Angie Wallace, who also owns Pure Indulgence Spa at the Divi Aruba Phoenix Beach Resort. All of her spas are open to the public and are very popular with locals. ✉ *J. E. Irausquin Blvd. 45, Druif* ☎ *297/583–0083 ext. 5298 (Divi), 297/582–0752 ext. 5298 (Tamarijn)* ⊕ *spaaruba.com.*

Mandara Spa

SPAS | Mandara Spa was created with a Balinese theme and offers specialty Indonesian-style treatments that incorporate the *boreh* (a traditional warm healing pack of special spices) followed by an Aruba-inspired wrap using local aloe and cucumber. The menu lists a wide variety of skin and body treatments for both women and men, and there's a full-service hair and nail salon, ideal for

Did You Know?

Aruba native Sarah-Quita Najive Offringa started windsurfing at age 9 at Fisherman's Hut Beach. Since then, she has won more than 20 world championship titles.

a wedding party. Honeymooners and couples will appreciate special packages that include private couple's treatment rooms, extra-large whirlpool baths, and Vichy showers. ⊠ *Mariott's Aruba Ocean Club, L. G. Smith Blvd. 101, Palm Beach* ☎ *297/520–6750* ⊕ *www.mandaraspa.com.*

Okeanos Spa

SPAS | The full-service spa at the Renaissance Wind Creek Aruba Resort is well equipped to help you relax to the max, but the incredible seaside palapa cove on private Renaissance Island is the best venue for a relaxing couple's massage or a signature treatment. It's accessible by free water taxi when you book a treatment, and your purchase also gains you access to the private island. Access to the island is otherwise limited to resort guests. There are beach bars, lounge service, and a full-service restaurant on-site, so you can make an entire blissful day of it. ⊠ *Renaissance Aruba Resort & Casino, L. G. Smith Blvd. 82, Oranjestad* ☎ *297/583–6000* ⊕ *www.marriott.com/hotels/travel/auabr-renaissance-wind-creek-aruba-resort/.*

★ Pure Indulgence Spa

SPAS | This gorgeous, glassed-in multilevel spa has the island's only sea-view mani-pedi treatment room (the loft) and has been recently renovated to include an inviting outdoor terrace lounge as a spot to sip your welcome mimosas upon arrival. The Pure Couple's Escape signature treatment includes massage and time spent in a private Lover's Suite replete with whirlpool baths, a steam room, and premium Hansgrohe rain showers. They also offer hot stone and prenatal treatments and a wide range of facials and body renewal packages. ∎**TIP➜ For a real treat, book a massage on the beach in their outdoor cabana just steps from the sea.** ⊠ *Divi Aruba Phoenix Beach Resort, J. E. Irausquin Blvd. 75, Palm Beach* ☎ *297/586–6066* ⊕ *www.facebook.com/pureindulgencespa* ⊗ *Closed Sun.*

Purun Spa

SPAS | Reflecting the kind of upscale elegance and high-quality services one would expect of a spa located in adults-only luxury boutique Bucuti & Tara Beach Resort, this oasis of pampering offers a wide range of unique treatments with a focus on natural products and holistic health and wellness. There's also an outdoor cabana for massages and services. It's open to the public, but reservation preferences are given to resort guests. ⊠ *Bucuti & Tara Beach Resort, L. G. Smith Blvd. 55B, Eagle Beach* ☎ *297/583–1100 ext. 120* ⊕ *www.bucuti.com/wellness/spa* ⊿ *From $149* ⊗ *Closed Sun.*

Many Aruba resorts have their own spas providing body treatments and massages.

★ The Ritz-Carlton Spa

SPAS | Upscale pampering and top-notch service is the hallmark of this massive 15,000-foot emporium with 13 treatment rooms, a full-service salon, soothing indoor his-and-hers water therapy pools, saunas, steam rooms, an oxygen bar, and a boutique. Signature treatments feature local island ingredients like aloe and coffee (for scrubs), and there's a good selection of treatments for men. Their "Body Reset" treatment is ideal for arrival to combat jet lag, and the "Divi Divi" massage is not to be missed—it was specially developed by their own local therapists incorporating a variety of soothing techniques and oil derived from the local watapana (divi-divi) tree. ⊠ *The Ritz-Carlton, Aruba, L. G. Smith Blvd. 107, Palm Beach* ☎ *297/527–2525* ⊕ *www.ritzcarlton.com/en/hotels/auart-the-ritz-carlton-aruba/spa/* ✉ *From $125.*

Spa del Sol

SPAS | An ideal Zen sanctuary right on the sea—and a partner to Manchebo's extensive health, wellness, and yoga services and retreats—this Balinese-themed spa hosts a bevy of partly open-air treatment rooms so you can hear the relaxing sounds of the waves. A full range of treatments is available, including couple's massages. ⊠ *Manchebo Beach Resort and Spa, J. E. Irausquin Blvd. 55, Manchebo Beach* ☎ *297/582–6145* ⊕ *www.spadelsol. com* ☉ *Closes at 2pm Sundays.*

ZoiA Spa

SPAS | This luxurious full-service oasis named after the Papiamento word for "balance" offers treatments indoor and out and focuses on using Aruba's natural resources for rejuvenation as much as possible. Some unique signature treatments take place right in the water in the adult-only Trankilo pool, facing the sea. New treatments include Aruba Sun Rescue using local aloe vera, and ZoiA Bon Bini (meaning "welcome") for deep stress-relieving effects that includes foot reflexology after massage. Express mani-pedis are also very popular, and they offer a full range of hair care in their salon, too. ⊠ *Hyatt Regency Aruba Beach Resort, Spa, and Casino, J. E. Irausquin Blvd. 85, Palm Beach* ☎ *297/586–1234* ⊕ *www.hyatt.com/en-US/spas/Zoia-Spa/home.*

Submarine Excursions

★ Atlantis Submarines

ENTERTAINMENT CRUISE | FAMILY | Enjoy the deep without getting wet in a real U.S. Coast Guard–approved submarine with *Atlantis,* run by De Palm Tours. The underwater reefs are teeming with marine life, and the 65-foot air-conditioned sub takes up to 48 passengers for a voyage 130 feet into the deep to view shipwrecks and amazing sights with informative narration. The company also owns the *Seaworld Explorer,* a semisubmersible that allows passengers to sit and view Aruba's marine habitat from 5 feet below the surface. ⊠ *Renaissance Marina, L. G. Smith Blvd. 82, Oranjestad* ☎ *297/522–4400* ⊕ *depalm.com/submarine-tours* 🎟 *Sub from $114; Seaworld Explorer from $55* ⌖ *Children must be a minimum of 36 inches tall and 4 years old for the submarine.*

Windsurfing and Kiteboarding

Aruba has ideal conditions for windsurfing: trade winds that average 20 knots year-round and calm azure-blue waters. With a few lessons from a certified instructor, even novices will be jibing in no time. The southwestern coast's tranquil waters at Fisherman's Huts make it ideal for both beginners and intermediates, as the winds are steady and sudden gusts are rare. Experts will find Grapefield and Boca Grandi beaches more challenging; winds are fierce and often shift without warning.

The same wind and water conditions are also ideal for kiteboarding, and though it takes longer to learn, it has become almost as popular. This sport involves gliding on and above the water on a small surfboard or wakeboard while hooked up to a kite. Windsurfing experience helps and practice time on the beach is essential, but these are different sports. You can watch the colorful kites

Did You Know?

Near-constant trade winds that average 20 knots have made Aruba a popular windsurfing destination. The conditions at Fisherman's Huts Beach (a.k.a. Hadicurari) make it one of the world's best places to learn the sport.

flying all around Fisherman's Huts Beach, where boarders practice and give lessons. Pros will tell you to carve out at least four hours for your first lesson on the beach. And the past few years, the newer sport of "wing foiling" has officially taken flight on the island, too. It's a surfboard with a fin (foil) attached to the bottom of it, and a handheld sail gives you the power to slice through the waves. Bizarre, but fun.

Each year, usually in July, the Hi-Winds Pro-Am Windsurfing Competition attracts professionals and amateurs from around the world. The event has become one big weeklong beach party with entertainment that goes day and night. You don't need to be a boarder to enjoy it.

★ Aruba Active Vacations

WATER SPORTS | FAMILY | Located on Fisherman's Huts Beach—the best spot on the island for optimum wind and wave conditions—this operation has been the go-to for many years as THE best place to learn windsurfing, kiteboarding, and, more recently, wing foiling. Local alums of their school include world-class competitors like Women's Windsurf Champion Sarah-Quita Offringa, and their expert instructors ensure even first-timers are riding the waves in no time. They also offer mountain biking and stand-up paddleboarding, and they are the only outfit on the island that does "blokarting"—sail-powered land carting. ⊠ L. G. Smith Blvd. 486, Palm Beach ⊹ On Fisherman's Huts Beach ☎ 297/586–0989 ⊕ aruba-active-vacations.com ⊠ From $60.

★ Vela Aruba

WINDSURFING | FAMILY | All kinds of sporty fun-in-the-sun options are available at this funky kiosk in the sand, including professional windsurfing and kiteboarding lessons; they are the first official operator to offer "wing foiling" lessons. You can rent sea kayaks and stand-up paddleboards (and take lessons in both). Instructors even offer yoga and Pilates on stand-up paddleboards. Snorkel equipment rental and "Zayak" sea sleds (floats with transparent windows to see the marine life below) are also available, as are beach boot camp classes. ⊠ L. G. Smith Blvd. 101, Palm Beach ⊹ Between the Aruba Marriott and the Ritz-Carlton ☎ 297/586–3735 ⊕ www.velaaruba.com ⊠ Rentals from $35; lessons from $60.

Index

Photo Credits

Front Cover: Jon Arnold Images Ltd/Alamy Stock Photo [**Description:** Caribbean, Netherland Antilles, Aruba, Baby beach]. **Back cover, from left to right:** Littleny Stock/Shutterstock. Littleny Stock/Shutterstock. Chiyacat/Shutterstock. **Spine:** Vilainecrevette/Shutterstock. **Interior, from left to right:** MasterPhoto/Shutterstock (1). David Troeger/Aruba Tourism Authority (2-3). **Chapter 1: Experience Aruba:** Aruba Tourism Authority (6-7). Littleny Stock/Shutterstock (8-9). Göran Ingman/Flickr (9). Corey Weiner/Red Square, Inc. (9). Aruba Mural Tours (10). Max Broenink/Shutterstock (10). Bambi2020/Shutterstock (10). Mulevich/Shutterstock (10). Aruba Tourism Authority (11). Aruba Tourism Authority (11). Aruba Tourism Authority (12). Meunierd/Shutterstock (12). Rob Arismendi (12). Courtesy of Kukoo Kunuku (12). Mihai_Andritoiu/Shutterstock (13). Grand Aruba Spa/Flickr (13). Artn Photography (16). Aruba Tourism Authority (16). Jetlag Creative Studio (16). Aruba Tourism Authority (16). Aruba Tourism Authority (17). Tierra Del Sol (18). Aruba Tourism Authority (18). Cado de Lannoy/Aruba Active Vacations (18). Aruba Tourism Authority (18). Aruba Tourism Authority (19). The Aruba Tourism Authority (20). Ami Wall (21). **Chapter 3: Oranjestad:** Dbvirago/iStockphoto (59). Birdiegal/Shutterstock (64). Mel Gonzalez/Shutterstock (66-67). Kenneth Theysen/Timeless-Pixx (71). Aruba Made (75). Littleny Stock/Shutterstock (81). Ildi Papp/Shutterstock (84). **Chapter 4: Manchebo, Druif, And Eagle Beaches:** Kjersti Joergensen/Dreamstime (87). Fmbackx/iStockphoto (92-93). Amsterdam Manor Beach Resort Aruba (101). Bucuti Beach Resort (102). **Chapter 5: Palm Beach and Noord and Western Tip (California Dunes):** DiegoMariottini/Shutterstock (107). Hans Wagemaker/Shutterstock (116). Serge Yatunin/Shutterstock (121). Corey Weiner/Red Square, Inc. (126). Agenturfotografin/Shutterstock (134). Susan Campbell (136). Littleny Stock/Shutterstock (138-139). **Chapter 6: San Nicolas and Savaneta:** Aruba Tourism Authority (141).Susan Campbell (146). Kjersti Joergensen/Shutterstock (148). Frankie Calkins/Shutterstock (153). Steve Photography/Shutterstock (156). **Chapter 7: Arikok National Park and Environs:** Aruba Tourism Authority (159). Aruba Tourism Authority (167). Aruba Tourism Authority (168). Paul D'Innocenzo (172-173). **Chapter 8: Activities:** Steve Photography/Shutterstock (175). Corey Weiner/Red Square, Inc. (177). Corey Weiner/Red Square, Inc. (180). Susan Campbell (182). Courtesy of Marriott (185). Rebecca Genin/Aruba Tourism (188). Armando Goedgedrag (194-195). Scott Lowden/Aruba Tourism Authority (197). Paul D'Innocenzo (199). **About Our Writers:** All photos are courtesy of the writers except for the following. *Every effort has been made to trace the copyright holders, and we apologize in advance for any accidental errors. We would be happy to apply the corrections in the following edition of this publication.